THE

Tailgater's

COOKBOOK

Also by David Joachim

FRESH CHOICES

BRILLIANT FOOD TIPS AND COOKING TRICKS

A MAN, A CAN, A PLAN

A MAN, A CAN, A GRILL

A MAN, A CAN, A MICROWAVE

THE
Tailgater's
COOKBOOK

David Joachim

BROADWAY BOOKS

NEW YORK

PRINTED IN THE UNITED STATES OF AMERICA

BROADWAY BOOKS and its logo, a letter B bisected on the diagonal, are trademarks of Random House, Inc.

Visit our Web site at www.broadwaybooks.com

First edition published 2005

Book design by Vertigo Design, NYC

Library of Congress Cataloging-in-Publication Data

Joachim, David.
　　The tailgater's cookbook / David Joachim.—1st ed.
　　　　p.　cm.
　　Includes index.
　　　1. Outdoor cookery.　2. Picnicking.　3. Tailgate parties.　I. Title.

TX823.J43 2005
641.5'78—dc22

　　　　　　　　　　　　　　　　　　　　　2004062259

ISBN 0-7679-1835-5

10　9　8　7　6　5　4　3　2　1

For August and Maddox

Contents

THE
Tailgater's
COOKBOOK

Introduction:
CHILLIN' AND GRILLIN' IN AMERICA

WHAT IS IT THAT DRAWS THOUSANDS OF PEOPLE TO STAND AROUND ON ASPHALT, sometimes in the bitter cold and rain? Is it the infectious enthusiasm of fans in team colors? The spectacle of hilarious costumes and outlandish vehicles? The wafting warmth of a charcoal fire? The vast array of tables spread with every kind of food imaginable from the chilled to the grilled?

I've tailgated at football games, soccer matches, car races, and even in the parking lots of theme parks and ski resorts. In my broad definition of the experience, you can tailgate anywhere you're allowed to park your car, grill food, and enjoy a drink with friends. But tailgating means different things to different people. Whenever I go to a tailgate party, I ask people what it means to them. What's it all about? Why do people invest so much time and money on the place where you park your car before heading into the event?

The answers are all over the map. For a lot of people, it's all about team spirit. It's about being a good fan and supporting the players and the team. Take the Boneshaker, for example, better known as Mike Parisi. He's been a Tampa Bay Buccaneers season-ticket holder for more than ten years. Mike fires up the football players and fans at every home game. He has a ship tattooed on one leg and a Bucs flag tattooed on the other. He wears a custom-made Bucs earring and matching necklace. Mike also brings an eighty-pound rattling wooden boneshaker to every game. Mike the Boneshaker lives to get the team pumped up to win.

Farther north, there's Titanman, a die-hard Tennessee Titans fan. Also known as David Anderson, Titanman has been dressing up like Captain America for more than five years. In full superhero regalia, Titanman is the team's warrior. He plays the theme music from the movie *Rocky* to rally the troops to victory. And like any good superfan, Titanman trash-talks the competition whenever they enter the Coliseum in Nashville.

Look around any stadium parking lot and you'll notice that some of the most devoted fans are women. Stephanie Phillips has held season tickets to Philadelphia Eagles games for more than fifteen years. On game day, she usually gets up at six A.M. to finish making the mountains of food she began preparing days before; she drives forty-five minutes to the stadium; and she's tailgating by nine A.M. At work, at home, at games, Stephanie is an Eagles fanatic. Her mailbox, bathroom, den, and guest room are completely decked out in Eagles green.

Then there's Len Orme, a Cincinnati Bengals season-ticket holder since 1980 who has never missed a home game. Len, a longtime fan, has his van painted in Bengals colors—black with orange stripes. His entire basement enshrines the Bengals with an endless display of team memorabilia. Len wears a simple orange and black tiger hat to every game. A model of the tailgater's generous spirit, Len has raised more than $25,000 for the underprivileged and homeless in Cincinnati at the annual Bengals Dance fund-raiser.

All four of these loyal fans were recently inducted into the Visa Hall of Fans at the Pro Football Hall of Fame in Canton, Ohio. Established in 1998, the Hall of Fans pays tribute to folks like these who go all out to support their favorite NFL team. Check out more of the crazy costumes and decked-out vehicles of the most dedicated football fans in personal profiles throughout this book.

TAILGATING IS A PARTY

THERE'S NO DOUBT THAT SPORTS FANS ARE THE LIFEBLOOD OF TAILGATING. Their enthusiasm helps spur players and teams to victory and embraces them in defeat. Fans have long been considered the "Twelfth Man" of the football team, a tradition begun in 1922 at Texas A&M University (see page 4 for more history on the Twelfth Man).

But tailgating isn't only about team spirit. The most raucous revelers say it's all about the party, dude! It's about having a good time. Getting pumped! Psyched! Raging! Some tailgaters hire a live band or DJ to get the party rockin'. Others truck in wide-screen TVs, satellite dishes, and huge sound systems to start things up. Russ Stevenson, better known as Tailgate Russ, goes one step further. He's got the music and the food, but he's also been known to hire a world-renowned sand sculptor for tailgate parties. Russ used to tailgate at Eagles home games until his parties got too complicated for stadium officials. No problem. Tailgate Russ took his show on the road. Now he stages not parties but *events* at Eagles games around the country. The first of these events was held in Jacksonville, Florida, featuring two live bands, a DJ, four masseuses, an Elvis impersonator, and eight hundred guests. Now, that's a tailgate party!

Tailgate Russ easily surpassed his original goal of staging a tailgate with one thousand people. In December 2003 at a Miami racecourse, Tailgate Russ presided over two thousand tailgaters before the Eagles/Dolphins game. His current goal? To become a full-time event planner. Sounds like you're well on your way, Russ.

DRINK UP!

TAILGATE PARTIES TAKE ON ALL SORTS OF THEMES, usually rooted in the team's colors, mascot, or region. But stop by any sports tailgate and you can't help but notice one common

---

The Twelfth Man

January 2, 1922, marks a milestone in the history of tailgating. That's the day that fans were recognized as an integral part of the team. It's the day that tailgaters became the "Twelfth Man" on the field, supporting and serving their favorite football team.

On that day, at Texas A&M University, former football player E. King Gill was up in the press box helping reporters to get the names of the players correct. Down on the field, the A&M Aggies were up against Centre College, the nation's top-ranked team. As the game became fierce, the underdog Aggies were running out of good players. The coach, Dana X. Bible, remembered that Gill was a former football player. Coach Bible called Gill from the press box and got him suited up. Gill stood ready on the sideline. The game continued and the Aggies finally won in a 22–14 upset. At the end of the game, Gill was the only man left on the Aggies sideline.

Gill had accepted the call to help the team. According to A&M history, "that spirit of readiness for service, desire to support, and enthusiasm helped kindle a flame of devotion among the entire student body; a spirit that has grown vigorously throughout the years. The entire student body at A&M is the Twelfth Man, and they stand during the entire game to show their support."

Although Gill did not play in the game, he sparked a tradition of team devotion that continues to this day. For many tailgaters, that spirit is what brings them to the stadium throughout the season to cheer on and support their team. Both the fans and the players know that team spirit is what the home field advantage is all about.

thread. Beer. In cans, in cups, in kegs, in funnels . . . it's everywhere you want to be. Tailgaters love to drink beer—or any alcohol, for that matter. While some say tailgating is all about the party, others get more specific and say that it's really about beer.

Teetotalers take note: drinking has a long tradition in tailgating, which dates back to the first college football games ever played. "Back then, Americans drank to an extent that we'd find kind of shocking today. At those games in the 1880s and 1890s, there are accounts of students getting rowdy and throwing empty liquor bottles at the police around the field . . . there was a lot of alcohol," says Mark Bernstein, author of *Football: The Ivy League Origins of an American Obsession*. Way back in 1869, at the very first football game between Rutgers and Princeton, students met before the game to drink and socialize, adds Bernstein. And so a tailgating ritual was born.

That same tradition is alive and kicking today. Just ask Sean Deegan, a member of the New York Jets tailgate squad dubbed Troop 16H. "On any given weekend, we'll go through ten half-kegs of beer," says Deegan. For a suggested twenty-dollar dona-

Suds Go Way Back

For beer-lovers, it's hard to imagine watching sports without it. Fortunately, sports fans have never had to: beer has been around a *really* long time. Here are some highlights.

- The oldest known beer recipe dates back to ancient Sumer, about 6,000 B.C. Back then, spectators drank a brew made of partially baked bread mixed with water, cumin, ginger, and other spices.

- The Sumerians had a goddess of beer named Ninkasi.

- According to Sumerian beliefs, beer was associated with females. Sumerian brewers and tavern owners were all women.

- In the 5,000-year-old *Epic of Gilgamesh*, the key character Enkidu is told to "drink the beer, as is the custom of the land."

After drinking seven jugs, he "became expansive and sang with joy. He was elated and his face glowed. . . . He put on some clothing and became like a warrior."

- According to clay tablets found in what is now Iraq, Noah stocked up the ark with beer.

- Native Americans were making beer using corn and tree sap before Columbus arrived.

- The Yuengling Brewery, located in Pottsville, Pennsylvania, was founded in 1829. It's the oldest operating brewery in America.

tion, the troop hosts huge parties of up to 250 thirsty fans in what the *New York Post* calls "the mother of all tailgate bashes." Gallon after gallon of suds flows from two beer taps fitted in the side of the troop's Vietnam-era military transporter (which is painted Jets green, of course).

Go to any big football game, like the Orange Bowl, and you'll witness a similar scene: truckloads of psyched-up fans drinking like there's no tomorrow. Vodka, rum, tequila, whiskey . . . almost every kind of liquor makes its appearance. But beer still reigns supreme as the ultimate tailgater fuel. Just be smart about it: always party with a designated driver.

FAN FEAST

BEER MAY BE A BIG DRAW AT TAILGATE PARTIES EVERYWHERE, but the food is equally alluring, if not more so. How could anyone resist the wafting aroma of slow-smoked Texas beef brisket? Or the sweet and sticky lip-smack of Kansas City ribs? The spicy voodoo of a big ol' pot of Louisiana gumbo? Or the snap of bratwurst grilled until the skin is crisp, then served on a crusty roll slathered with grainy mustard and grilled onions and peppers?

Tailgate food runs the gamut from store-bought chips and dip to dry-rubbed grilled steaks to whole roasted suckling pig. Serious tailgaters spare no expense when it comes to laying out a great spread. The more extravagant arrive in limousines, hire professional chefs, and dine on fine food like caviar and champagne. The do-it-your-selfers may drag entire pizza ovens to the parking lot and power them with electric generators. Meanwhile, dedicated tailgate cooks will truck in big barbecue pits and slow-cook whole hogs all day the traditional way over smoldering wood for a communal pig pickin' after the game.

Most tailgaters make do with what they have (and dream about getting more). They cook on everything from cut-up and re-welded fifty-gallon drums to old burned-out car hoods. Pinto Ron, a.k.a. Ken Johnson, cooks his tailgate food on the hood of a modified 1980 Pinto that he drives to Ralph Wilson Stadium for Buffalo Bills home games. He cooks pancakes on a hot shovel, hamburgers on a metal rake, and pizzas in the upper drawer of an old metal filing cabinet. That's quite a spectacle on game day.

Every stadium parking lot has its favorite regional foods. At Ohio State University, you'll spot buckeye candies made from peanut butter and chocolate in various shapes and sizes. Go to a Buffalo Bills game and you'll taste the local specialty of roast beef sandwiches known as beef on weck. Steaming Cincinnati chili fills the bowls at Bengals games. Beer brats are king in Green Bay. And if you go to the NFL stadiums in St. Louis, Kansas City, or Houston, you'll feast on some of the best barbecue tailgating has to offer.

Of course, plenty of fans stick with the basics: a cooler and a small portable grill. Hamburgers and hot dogs are mainstays of American tailgating. But seasoned fans seek out higher thrills from the grill. Wander around the parking lot and you're bound to come across everything from bison steaks to elk burgers to venison chops over the coals.

I have to admit, I'm in it for the grilled food. The sheer diversity of tailgate fare makes it a feast like no other. But for my money, the grilled food is where it's at. Without a grill, a tailgate is merely a picnic. In my mind, grilling and barbecuing are what make tailgating a uniquely American phenomenon. You don't see too much grilling at Le Tour de France. Wine and cheese, yes. Barbecued baby-back ribs, no.

Only in America has grilling evolved into such a distinctive and popular cooking method. In fact, some of the most detailed descriptions of barbecuing appear in early American cookbooks, particularly those from the South. The widely used Weber kettle grill was invented in America. And with the rise of convenient gas grills, barbecues remain a national pastime clear across the country. Eighty-one percent of Americans own home grills and more than half of us grill food all year long, according to the Hearth, Patio, and Barbecue Association.

THE GRIDIRON COMMUNITY

SUFFICE IT TO SAY THAT GRILLING AND AMERICAN SPORTS WILL ALWAYS GO TOGETHER. Some early American cookbooks describing barbecue even refer to the grill rack as a "gridiron." Nowadays, the gridiron usually means the football field. And that's exactly what brings together the American traditions of football and grilling. The gridiron is both the American football field and the American pastime of gathering around the grill for a barbecue. Tailgating is the game within the game. The spectacle in the parking lot mirrors the one played out on the football field. Just as football teams battle to win, so do the fans duke it out in the parking lot. Tailgaters often compete to see who has the best team spirit, the best tailgate party, the biggest grill, the most outrageous tailgating vehicle, and the best food.

In its broadest definition, tailgating is about encouraging this sense of community. It's about getting together to enjoy some quality time with your friends or family. Think about it. Where else can thousands of Americans meet to hang out these days? As town centers and public meeting places have been replaced by office buildings, shops, and residential developments, there are few places left for large groups of people to gather. The open-air parking lots of sports stadiums are the rare exception.

According to Joe Cahn, a professional tailgater known as the Commissioner of Tailgating, "it's the new community social." Since 1996, Joe and his cat Sophie have tailgated from their Monaco Motorcoach in parking lots all over the country. In 2002, Coca-Cola sponsored Joe's study of this growing American pastime. Since then, the Commish has logged more than 200,000 miles, visited more than 90 stadiums, and surveyed over 1,200 tailgaters. In his 2003 State of Tailgating Report, Joe sums up the phenomenon this way: "In today's society, people yearn for socialization and the parking lot provides the perfect place for everyone to come together. It's a place where no one locks their doors and everyone is happy to see you." Amen, brother. According to the Commish, "tailgating is the last great American neighborhood."

Whether it's about the party, the beer, the food, or the community, one thing is for sure: tailgating is huge. According to the American Tailgaters Association (ATA), more than 20 million tailgaters party in parking lots across the country every year. The makers of Weber grills put that figure even higher, estimating that more than 36 million Americans tailgate through the year. The highest expression of tailgating happens at college and pro football games. But NASCAR races account for about 20 percent of tailgating, according to the ATA. And baseball games account for about 17 percent of tailgating, according to Weber-Stephen Products. I'd go one step further and say that *anytime* you have people gathered together, chillin' and grillin' near the vehicle they drove there, you have tailgating. It could happen at a football game, a baseball game, a car race, a soccer match, or a music festival.

The Tailgater's Cookbook is about sharing this great American pastime with you. Inside, you'll find recipes and tips for tailgating in all its wonderful guises. The recipes were collected from and inspired by tailgaters around the country. People like Big John Gavin, a Houston Texans fan, shared his recipe for baked eggs with sausage, cheese, and chiles (page 154). And Mike Hammett, a member of the Raider Nation, inspired me to develop the recipe for Tequila Tri-Tip (page 86). Quite a few of the recipes are my take on tailgate favorites enjoyed by loyal football fans in different regions around the country.

I assume that you can get things like a standard mayonnaise-based potato salad recipe from family, friends, or the Internet. Or, hell, you could just go to the store and buy some prepared potato salad. What I aim to give you here is something different. A Red, White, and Blue Potato Salad (page 44). Beer and Coffee Steaks (page 84). Chipotle-Bourbon Ribs (page 74). And Grilled Stuffed French Toast (page 110). You'll see both breakfast and dessert recipes for tailgaters who like to come early and stay late.

A Note on the Recipes

Whenever I plan a tailgate menu, I think, "We'll need something big for the grill" or "We need a salad or something cold from the cooler." I try to make sure I don't overfill the grill or plan so many cold foods that they won't fit in the cooler. So that's how I organized the recipes in this book—by tailgate foods located In the Cooler, On the Grill, Out of the Pot, From the Thermos, and In the Bag. This way of organizing the recipes lets you know what kind of equipment you'll need at the tailgate. If you're not planning to bring a grill, you can skip the recipes in the Grill chapter. (But, c'mon, you've *got* to grill. It's the heart of tailgating!)

Hopefully this sort of broad-stroke chapter arrangement will make it easier to round out your tailgate menus. But if you're looking for something more specific like a sandwich, a beef main dish, or a dessert, check out the recipe lists at the beginning of each chapter. These lists give you a sneak peek at the recipes within each chapter and include more conventional food categories like dips, spreads, sandwiches, salads, starters, soups, stews, beef, pork, chicken, seafood, desserts, cold drinks, hot drinks, etc. If you have any trouble finding what you're looking for, check the mother lode of lists: the index at the back of the book.

You'll also find plenty of tailgate standards like Brats in Beer (page 68), Barbecued Chicken (page 94), and Championship Chili (page 130). I include a range of recipes for every kind of tailgater. Some folks have been tailgating for decades, perfecting the art and dedicating loads of time and money to the food. Others are just starting out and are perfectly happy with grilled burgers and dogs. This book provides recipes and tips for making your tailgate party better and better every time—whether it's your first or your fiftieth. And if you're not the one doing the actual cooking, you can always share the recipes with those handling the food.

I also toss in a bunch of trivia tidbits throughout the book so you can impress your parking lot pals. What's a tailgate party without a little showing off? Cheers!

THE
Tailgater's
TOOLKIT

EXPERIENCED TAILGATERS ARE EASY TO SPOT. They're the ones sitting in comfortable chairs, beer in hand, plateful of food nearby, thoroughly enjoying the party. They make it look easy. These are the calm and confident folks who, just moments ago, served up multiple racks of succulent, hickory-smoked, mahogany-colored baby-back ribs; roasted ears of savory, spice-rubbed corn; and big bowls of sassy-tasting, crunchy coleslaw to dozens of ravenous tailgaters. They're the impresarios of the tailgate party.

Just like quarterbacks on the field, these seasoned tailgate cooks have their secret weapons. They have a culinary playbook filled with tricks that make them the MVPs of the day. Sometimes it's a cool tool like a rib rack to save space on the grill. Other times it's a handy technique like using wood chips on a gas grill for more flavor. Here's a look inside the playbook of the smart tailgate cook.

BEFORE YOU GO

SURE, YOU COULD JUST HIRE A CATERER, BUT THAT'S CHEATING. Tailgating is all about making a home away from home. Making a whole world in your little corner of the parking lot. To make the job easier, follow the old Boy Scout rule of thumb: be prepared. Do as much as you can before getting to the tailgate. Make a list, dole out tasks to others coming to the tailgate, and pack up at least a day ahead. Prepare as much food as you can ahead of time. Most salads, soups, dips, sauces, and desserts can be completely prepared ahead. Even main dishes and side dishes can be mostly prepared before the game. Hamburgers can be shaped. Steaks, chops, and poultry can be marinated or spice-rubbed. Veggies can be trimmed, cut, and sealed in bags or airtight containers. When you get to the tailgate, all you should have to do is grill or reheat the food, grab a beer, and set things out for everyone to enjoy.

Here's some other basic know-how for putting on a good party. If you've been tailgating for several seasons, you may want to skip down to the more advanced tips in the section "When You Get There" beginning on page 22.

SIZE IT UP. The size of your tailgate will determine almost everything else you need to know. How many people will you be feeding? How much tailgate space will you have? If it's just you and a couple buddies out for some easy eats and drinks

The Tailgater's Big Checklist

Tailgating is kind of like car camping. You need most of the same stuff—except maybe flashlights and sleeping bags. But if you're planning to party into the night, bring those, too! Here's a list of basics and cool extras that covers just about everything you'll need to enjoy a great party. Skip whatever items you know you won't need. Or divide up the items among other people coming to the tailgate.

Basics

GENERAL STUFF

Tickets

Team hat, shirt, flag, or other merchandise

Sunglasses, sunblock, and cool footwear (warm weather)

Gloves, hat, coat, warm footwear, and blanket (cold weather)

Umbrella and rain gear

Chairs

Folding table

Tarp and poles, or other shelter

FOOD AND DRINK STUFF

Food cooler

Drinks cooler

Carry-all bag

Ice

Water

Liquor, wine, or drink mixers

Buns or bread

Condiments

Seasonings

Chips or other salty snacks

Cookies or other sweet snacks

GRILL STUFF

Grill

Charcoal

Newspaper or lighter cubes

Lighter or matches

Propane

Grill brush

Tongs

Spatula

Grill mitts or oven mitts

Disposable aluminum pans

Small metal trash can

SERVING AND CLEANUP STUFF

Knife

Cutting board

Can opener

Bottle opener

Corkscrew

Blender

Trash bags

Water for cleaning

Aluminum foil

Plastic wrap

Paper towels

Kitchen towels

Cups, plates, bowls, forks, spoons, knives

Serving spoons, ladles, etc.

Napkins

Toothpicks

FUN STUFF

Football, Frisbee, cards, Baggo game, or other games

Stereo and CDs

Cool Extras

GENERAL STUFF

Camera

Binoculars

Seat cushions

Beer cozies

Pop-up shelter or canopy

Table cover

Extra batteries

Generator

Television and antenna

Extension cords

AC adapter

Jumper cables

Lantern or flashlight

Toilet paper

First aid kit

Bug spray

Antacid

Aspirin or ibuprofen

Earplugs

FOOD AND DRINK STUFF

Extra food cooler

Extra drinks cooler

Extra ice

Flask

Thermos

Insulated coffee press or coffeemaker

Coffee and filters

Hot cocoa mix

GRILL STUFF

Chimney starter

Wood chips or chunks

Grill rake, shovel, or poker

Basting brush

Grill mop

Grill basket

Skewers

Rib rack

Vertical roaster

Spray bottle

Pots and pans

Heatproof silicone gloves

Instant-read thermometer

SERVING AND CLEANUP STUFF

Zipper-lock bags

Airtight containers

Dish soap

Wash basin

Sponge

Dish towels

Wet wipes

Extra knives

Extra cutting board

Twist-ties

FUN STUFF

Cigars

before the game, one parking space, a cooler, and a small portable grill may do the job. But most tailgaters shoot higher. Buy extra parking spaces or share spaces with others to get as much tailgating area as you need. Then plan your menu based on the number of people you'll feed (plus a few extra for good measure). To lighten the load, split up the menu: have some folks bring salads, snacks, or desserts; some bring drinks; others take care of the grillable goods. Either way, the size of the party will determine how many coolers and how much grill space you'll need. If you're new to tailgating, see what kinds of basic supplies you may already have, like coolers, chairs, and a grill. Buy new gear based on how big your average tailgate is likely to be. See "The Tailgater's Big Checklist" (page 13) for a full list of amenities you might enjoy having at the tailgate.

BRING A TABLE OR TWO. Bring at least one folding table so you have somewhere to prep food and somewhere to serve it. For bigger parties, plan on having several tables. Table covers are a nice touch, especially if you can get them with team logos! See the sources for tailgating gear beginning on page 180.

THINK DISPOSABLE. Ceramic and glass may be nicer to eat and drink from, but they're a big chore to clean after the party. And chances for breakage go way up on the pavement. Use disposable cups, plates, bowls, forks, spoons, and knives. If you're worried about spills, buy extra-thick, good-quality disposable plastic plates and bowls. The more items you can throw away after the tailgate, the faster cleanup will be.

BUY A BIG STORAGE BIN. Keep your tailgating supplies in cheap plastic storage bins with tight-fitting lids. That way, you know where all your gear is, and you'll have one less thing to toss in the car. Look for a big bin (or a few smaller ones) in the camping gear section of your local home goods or sporting goods store. Restock the bin with things like paper products, trash bags, plastic dinnerware, and utensils when they begin to run low.

ZIP IT. I swear by zipper-lock bags for food prep and storage. Use them to hold marinated or spice-rubbed meats, pre-chopped veggies, seasoning mixes, salsas, and sauces. Toss the bags in your cooler or carry-all and you're ready to go. When they're empty, just toss the bags in the trash instead of having to clean another dirty dish. If you have extra food, put it in zipper-lock bags and bring it into the stadium. Or use the bags to dole out leftovers to your guests. I usually buy the thicker "freezer-weight" bags, since they're less prone to leaking. Stock up on several sizes: small (1-quart) for spice rubs and small foods; large (1 gallon) for most marinated meats; and extra large (2-gallon) for big cuts of meat like brisket and racks of ribs.

When making a marinade, mix the ingredients right in the bag to avoid dirtying any more dishes (I'm big on lightening up the cleaning load). Put the bag in a colander or bowl to help it stand upright. Fold down the top to help hold the bag open. Once the marinade ingredients are added, lift up the bag and give it a quick shake to mix the marinade (you don't have to dirty any spoons either!).

After you drop in the food, push out the air from the bag to make sure the marinade touches all surfaces of the food. Here's the easiest way: Wrap your hands tightly around the food while it's in the bag, then work your hands up from the food to the top of the bag, squeezing out the air as you go. When you reach the top of the bag, seal it from one corner to the other. Chill in the refrigerator or the cooler. Freezer-weight bags rarely leak, but to be absolutely safe, you can put the bag in a larger bag or dish to catch any dripped juices.

If you run out of zipper-lock bags, any leakproof, sturdy plastic bag can be used for marinating. Or use the traditional baking dish for marinating, but keep in mind that baking dishes will take up more room in your cooler.

PULL OUT THE OLD THERMOS. Years ago, when I was a carpenter, my stainless-steel thermos traveled with me every day. It brought me hot soup, cold drinks, and a portable cup and bowl. Now it does the same thing at tailgates. Thermoses are great for keeping cold drinks cold, hot soups hot, and freeing up more space in your cooler. If you'll be serving both hot soups and cold drinks, keep two thermoses on hand. For the recipes in this book, I use a 2-quart unbreakable steel thermos. Stanley makes one under the brand name Aladdin. It's a good investment; these things last a lifetime. You could also use two 1-quart thermoses instead. Look for steel thermoses instead of plastic. Steel doesn't stain or retain flavors like plastic can. And steer clear of glass-lined thermoses. They always break.

Get the most out of your thermos by pre-chilling or preheating it. To pre-chill, fill the container with ice and/or cold water and refrigerate the whole thing for at least 5 minutes. Dump out the ice water and fill with your cold drink. To preheat, fill the container with hot water, let it sit for at least 5 minutes, then dump out the water and pour in your hot drink or ladle in your soup or stew.

MULTIPLY YOUR COOLERS. For bigger tailgates (or even small ones), it helps to use at least two coolers: one for food and one for drinks. That way no one is knocking through your food to hunt down a beer. Buy extra coolers yourself or designate guests to bring the beer cooler or the food cooler. In the best of all possible worlds, you'll have several coolers on hand: two food coolers to separate the raw meats from the prepared foods; two drinks coolers to separate the beer from the other drinks; and another cooler just for ice.

DON'T SKIMP ON ICE. Bring plenty. You'll need most of it for the coolers, but you may also want some for filling drink cups. I usually fill the beer and drink coolers with ice only, but I also use ice packs in the food coolers. Unlike ice cubes, reusable ice packs don't melt into a watery mess and make your food soggy. I keep several sizes in my freezer, then layer some ice packs on the bottom of the food cooler, some in the middle, some on the sides, and some on top. If you need to keep foods cold overnight

Do Your Homework

I t's always a good idea to stay up on stadium rules while you're planning your tailgating party, whether you're a newcomer to the hobby or you're about to embark on another season. Here are some basic things to check out before you leave for the stadium.

- Are there designated tailgating lots? Is there RV parking? How much do parking spaces cost? Can you buy an extra space?
- When do the parking lots open before the game? Can you park a camper overnight?
- What are the rules on alcohol?
- Can you set up a tent?
- Can you have open flames, such as a bonfire?
- Are there restrictions on the kind of grills you can use?

- Can you operate a generator?
- Are there bathrooms or Porta Potties on the parking lot?
- Are there trash Dumpsters? Designated charcoal Dumpsters?

Joe Cahn zigzags across the country to game-day parties for a living. He recommends that when you're tailgating in an unfamiliar city, you check out the opposing team's official Web site first. The site will probably list the stadium's policies. You can also visit Cahn's Web site, www.tailgating.com, where he offers a page dedicated to tailgating groups for college and professional teams.

in your cooler, use both ice packs and ice cubes. Or pick up several jugs of water and freeze them before you go. Instant ice packs! Added bonus: if you need extra cold water at the tailgate, pull the jugs out of the cooler and let the ice melt.

BRING EXTRA FOOD SUPPLIES. Make sure you bring enough food for tail-gaters who may drop by (they always do—that's half the fun!) or tailgating neigh-bors you want to share food with. It's also a good idea to bring extra knives and cutting boards so others can help out with any last-minute food prep. To make cleanup go faster, bring an extra wash bucket and dish towels.

BEWARE THE WIND. Bring something heavy to hold down paper plates and napkins that might blow away in the breeze. If you have an E-Z Up tent or other pop-up shelter, tape a few filled water jugs to the bottom of the legs. These pop-up shelters are like huge umbrellas and can take off in a sudden gust of wind. Don't let your shelter ruin the tailgate next to you.

CHOOSE YOUR GRILL FUEL. For many tailgaters, grilling onsite is one of the main events of the tailgating experience. It doesn't matter whether you use gas or charcoal. Gas grills are more convenient, but charcoal gives you more flavor. It's your choice. I find that there's something more primal and fun about tending a fire instead of turning a knob. But that's just me. If you use charcoal briquettes, be sure

---

Ten No-Cook Foods to Pack in the Cooler

Tired of prepping food for the tailgate? Put some easy eats in your cooler so you can chill out and have a good time at the party.

1. Cold sandwiches like subs or heros from your favorite shop

2. Hummus and pita bread or crackers

3. Cold dips (bean dip, onion dip, salsa, sour cream, or blue cheese dip)

4. Assorted olives (or anything else from your supermarket's cold bar)

5. Roasted peppers

6. Veggies (cherry tomatoes, baby-cut carrots, celery sticks)

7. Fruit (grapes, apples, oranges)

8. Assorted cheeses (mozzarella, provolone, or your favorites)

9. Bagels and cream cheese

10. Peanut butter and jelly

to buy a good brand. Briquettes are made with varying mixtures of sawdust, wood scraps, and petroleum binders. Some burn more evenly and cleanly than others. I've found that national brands are more reliable than store brands. If you can, avoid using briquettes that are impregnated with lighter fluid. In fact, avoid lighter fluid altogether. It makes food taste like a gas tank. It's true that you can get away with using a little lighter fluid to start charcoal; that little bit of fluid will burn off before you put food over the coals. But the trouble is, no one ever uses a little. It's too much fun to pour it on and watch the flames begin!

See page 23 for tips on how to light charcoal quickly without resorting to lighter fluid. And if you like charcoal briquettes for their smokiness but don't like the added ingredients, give lump charcoal a try. Lump charcoal is made by charring real pieces of wood and that real wood is what lends great smoke flavor to grilled foods. Check your local hardware store or see the sources beginning on page 182 for lump charcoal. Of course, if you can, burning real wood logs, chunks, or chips will give you even more smoke flavor.

KEEP YOUR FUEL DRY. There's nothing worse than damp charcoal at a tailgate. Keep your grill fuel dry by storing it in plastic bags or buckets.

CARRY A SEPARATE GRILLING TOOLBOX. "Once you're out there, there's no running into the kitchen to get tongs or a basting brush," says Steven Raichlen, author of *The Barbecue Bible* and *How to Grill* (Workman Publishing) and other grilling cookbooks. Raichlen's advice? Use a tacklebox or toolbox to contain your grilling gear, including tongs, basting brush, spatulas, skewers, seasoning mixes, aluminum foil, and a roll of paper towels. "Bring a stack of aluminum foil pans for serving and cleanup," he says, "as well as a jug of water with a spigot on the front for handwashing."

SHOP TOP SHELF. Okay, you've got the basic gear, now what about the food? When buying food for your tailgate party, keep in mind that any dish you prepare will only be as good as your ingredients and your cooking techniques. So, first off, buy good ingredients! Yes, they sometimes cost more, but a good tailgate party is worth a couple extra bucks. To boost the flavor in foods you'll be grilling, use one or several of the following methods.

MARINATE. Marinades help to make grilled foods more tender and flavorful. They usually include oil, seasonings, and an acidic ingredient like vinegar, citrus juice, or

Tailgating Timeline

T he game's start time determines your timing for the tailgate. But here's what to do before and after the game, too. If you're a seasoned tailgater, you can probably get most things done the day before or the morning of the tailgate. If not, get a jump on things so you can relax and enjoy the party. And if you're tailgating somewhere new, find out when the stadium opens for parking and when you have to be outta there. That'll determine when you need to leave the house, how much time you have to set up your tailgate, and how much time there is for cooking, eating, and cleanup.

- **Weeks before:** Prepare make-ahead foods like Basic Tomato-Basil Sauce (page 117), Buckeye Candy (page 50), or other good keepers.

- **A week or few days before:** Plan menu (see page 172 for suggestions). Shop. Prepare make-ahead foods like Barbecue Beans (page 116), Chipotle Pecans (page 158), or other foods that can sit in the fridge for a week.

- **1 to 2 days before.** Prepare make-ahead foods like Spinach Artichoke Bread Bowl (page 36), Pesto Tortellini Salad (page 48), or other foods that can chill for a day or two before the tailgate. Marinate meats. Begin packing.

- **Day before:** Continue packing and food prep. Check items off your list as they're done.

- **Morning of tailgate:** Finish packing, prepping food, and loading up. Leave time to drive to the game and find parking.

- **3+ hours before start time:** Arrive at the stadium at least 3 hours before the start time if you plan to cook onsite and make it to the game. That leaves enough time to set up your tailgate, heat the grill, cook the food, eat, and clean up before you head in. Of course, you could arrive days ahead of time if regulations permit. Remember: the earlier you get there, the more time you have to relax.

- **1 to 2 hours before start time:** Eat, drink, and have fun! If you're not eating within an hour of start time, you're cutting it close. Leave time to cool down the grill, clean up, get into the stadium, and find your seats. Of course, if you're watching the game from the parking lot, just turn on your portable television and relax all day.

- **After the game:** Relax and munch some more. Clean up and leave your spot as you found it. Toss trash into Dumpsters before driving home.

buttermilk. The oil keeps food moist so it doesn't dry out on the grill; the seasonings add flavor; and the acid tenderizes food by breaking down some of its proteins. I usually marinate in freezer-weight zipper-lock bags because they help keep the marinade in direct contact with the food. And they're easy to transport to a tailgate. The big question is always: how long should foods marinate? The answer: times vary according to the strength of the marinade (how much seasoning and acid it contains) and the size and density of the food. Here's a good rule of thumb: Marinate really big or tough pieces of meat like brisket, pork shoulder, leg of lamb, whole turkeys, and wild-caught game for 12 hours or up to 2 days to penetrate or tenderize the meat. Large roasts like beef tenderloin, pork loin or tenderloin, and whole chickens can marinate for less time: 6 hours or overnight. Thick-cut steaks, chops, large whole fish, and small birds like Cornish hens benefit from 4 to 12 hours in a marinade. Thinner steaks and chops, lamb chops, bone-in poultry parts, and small whole fish get what they need in 2 to 6 hours. And boneless poultry parts, delicate fish fillets, shrimp, tofu, and vegetables can marinate for as little as 30 minutes or up to 2 hours. Recipes vary, though. The Chicken Spiedies recipe (page 92) traditionally marinates tender chicken breasts for 48 hours with great results! Experiment with marinades to find what works best for the food you're cooking. For more on marinade safety, see "Food Safety" on page 21.

INJECT. Marinades add flavor, but they really only penetrate about 1/8 to 1/4 inch into the surface of meats. If you want flavor all the way through a big piece of meat, inject it with the marinade instead of just soaking it in the marinade. Injecting is especially good for big pieces of meat that tend to dry out on the grill, like whole turkeys. To inject, buy a kitchen syringe (a.k.a. marinade injector) at a cookware store or well-stocked grocery store. Or see the sources beginning on page 182. These injectors look like oversize medical syringes and work the same way. You push the plunger down, insert the tip of the needle into the marinade, then slowly draw up the marinade into the syringe. Inject the marinade into the meat in several places, and voilà! Tenderized, flavor-filled meat. If you don't have a kitchen syringe, jab the meat in several places with a small sharp knife, then drop the meat into the marinade, working the marinade into the holes. It's not quite as good as injection, but a fair substitute. If your marinade includes chunks of food like onion or garlic, puree the marinade in a blender or food processor before drawing it into the injector.

BRINE. Brining is like marinating but with more water, more salt, and some added sugar. Brined meats usually soak longer, too—up to a week, depending on the meat's thickness. The benefit of brining is that it makes dry foods more moist and flavorful. It's a great technique for meats that tend to dry out on the grill like turkey and pork.

Food Safety

Common sense should follow you to the parking lot, especially when it comes to food. Use your noodle. Avoid letting food sit out on the table for hours and hours. When serving lots of food, bring it out in small batches, leaving things chilled in the cooler until you need them. Here are some other ways to eat safely in your favorite parking lot:

- **Stay clean.** Wash your hands in hot, soapy water before and after preparing food (particularly raw meat) and after using the rest room, changing diapers, or playing ball. Wash off your instant-read thermometer after testing grilled foods that will need further cooking.

- **Keep cold foods cold.** Refrigerate raw meats, poultry, and seafood in the store's packaging and put in a shallow pan to contain any juices. Use chilled meat, poultry, and seafood within 3 days, or freeze it. When defrosting foods, put them in a drip pan and defrost in the refrigerator rather than on countertops. Marinate meats, poultry, and seafood in the refrigerator unless marinating time is less than 1 hour. Use plenty of ice or ice packs to make sure meats, seafood, and eggs stay cold (40°F or lower) in your cooler until you're ready to cook them. Pack fish on ice to keep it as fresh as possible: put the ice in a colander, add the fish, and cover with a couple layers of plastic to keep everything contained, then put the filled colander in your cooler. While in transit, keep coolers inside the car if you can—rather than in the hot trunk—and put on the air conditioning. At the tailgate, keep the coolers in the shade if you can and avoid opening them too much. Replace ice as it melts. When cold food will be out for more than 2 hours, serve it on trays of ice to keep it chilled. If you have beer kegs, keep them iced down, out of the sun, and covered if possible. If you forget everything else, at least keep the beer cold!

- **Keep hot foods hot.** Cook foods to a safe temperature by using an instant-read thermometer (see recipes for doneness temperatures). Reheat leftovers to at least 165°F or bring soups, sauces, and stews to a boil. At the tailgate, serve pans or bowls of hot food on warming trays, in slow-cookers, or in chafing dishes. Or keep warm over a low-heat grill or burner.

- **Avoid cross-contamination.** Bacteria from raw foods can migrate to ready-to-eat foods. Use one cutting board for raw meats and a separate one for produce, breads, and other foods. When you only have one cutting board, cut produce and breads first, then raw meats and poultry. After prepping raw meat, wash cutting boards and other surfaces with hot, soapy water. Use disposable towels instead of sponges for soaking up spilled meat juices. (More good reasons to do as much prep at home as you can.) Marinate in heavy-duty zipper-lock bags or put bags of food in glass, ceramic, or other leakproof containers. After marinating meat and poultry, discard unused marinades or boil the used marinade for at least 2 minutes before serving. When using the marinade as a baste, set aside some of the marinade for this purpose before adding raw meat to the rest of the marinade; or boil used marinade for at least 1 minute before using as a baste or sauce. Use separate plates for cooked and raw foods. Avoid putting grilled food back onto the same plate that held raw meat or poultry.

- **When in doubt, throw it out.** Toss out any leftovers that have been at room temperature for more than 2 hours or in 90°F weather for more than an hour.

The salt in the brine opens up the proteins in the meat, which then draws in the brine's moisture and flavor. The result: flavorful meats that stay moist on the grill.

RUB. Spice rubs are the simplest flavoring technique for grilled and barbecued foods. Just shake on the spices, then grill or barbecue the food. Rubs also give meats a better crust than marinades because they're usually dry instead of wet. But rubs don't penetrate as much as marinades. For more flavors, I sometimes marinate meats first, then shake on a spice rub before grilling, as in Beer and Coffee Steaks (page 84). Other times, a good blend of seasonings on a great cut of meat is all you need, as in Smoky Rubbed Ribs (page 72). You can even mix your favorite spice rub into hamburgers to flavor up the meat. Rubs typically include salt, sugar, pepper, and other seasonings like garlic or onion powder, dill, cayenne pepper, bay leaf, or oregano. For foods that will spend less than 30 minutes over the heat, I like to shake the rub on 15 to 30 minutes before cooking so the seasonings have time to adhere to the food. But for meats that will cook for hours, like slow-grilled ribs, don't bother waiting. The seasonings will penetrate the food as it cooks. To see a variety of spice rubs, check out the recipes for Rum-Cardamom Pork Chops (page 70), Chipotle-Bourbon Ribs (page 74), Carolina Pulled Pork (page 77), Tequila Tri-Tip (page 86), Beer-Mopped Brisket with Texas Barbecue Sauce (page 88), Barbecued Chicken (page 94), and Beer-Butt Chicken (page 98).

BEHOLD THE CONDIMENT. Most people like to add their special flavor to food at the table. Bring along plenty of seasonings and condiments to get your guests involved in personalizing their food: salt and pepper, paprika, oregano, crushed red pepper flakes, Tabasco or other hot sauces, barbecue sauce, salsa, ketchup, mustard, mayonnaise . . . the sky's the limit.

WHEN YOU GET THERE

SETTING UP A TAILGATE IS A LOT LIKE SETTING UP CAMP. You find good places for the shelter, the tables, the chairs, and the grill. Then you get the party started! For me, that means firing up the grill and putting out a few munchies while the good stuff is over the coals. Here's a complete guide to successful tailgate grilling.

Most tailgaters use a home-style charcoal grill, whether a deep one, such as a Weber kettle grill, or a shallow one, such as a hibachi. But you could also use gas. If you're buying a new grill, check out "Get the Right Grill" on page 24.

For this book, I tested the recipes on the common 22-inch Weber kettle grill with a domed lid. I find the kettle grill to be the most versatile, simple, and satisfying grill for tailgates. Most of the directions in the grilled recipes are geared toward this type of covered grill. The recipes also include directions for cooking over gas.

For a complete list of basic and advanced grilling tools you might like to have, see the checklist on page 13. As for techniques, here's the play-by-play and some nifty tricks for great grilling every time.

LIGHT THE FIRE. If you're grilling over charcoal before the game, leave time to light the coals. With charcoal briquettes stacked in a pyramid among layers of newspaper (the old-fashioned way), it'll take about 30 minutes for hot coals. To speed things up, buy a chimney starter. Most hardware stores carry these cheap contraptions. They look like big, tall coffee cans with a divider near the bottom, holes in the sides, and a handle. You put the charcoal (lump or briquettes) in the top, some newspaper or paraffin lighter cubes in the bottom, and light the bottom. The upward draft of oxygen helps to light the coals faster. Typically, you get hot, ashy coals ready for cooking in about 15 minutes—half the time it takes with a pyramid. Pour out the coals, spread 'em evenly, and you're ready to grill.

Newspaper is the handiest fire starter, but cubes of paraffin are waterproof and light more reliably. Look for paraffin lighter cubes and chimney starters in hardware stores or home centers. Or check the barbecue sources beginning on page 182.

PREHEAT THE GRILL RACK. Once your fire is going, let the grill rack heat up for at least 10 minutes on high heat. A hot rack gives you a better sear on your food. When you're ready to grill, adjust the heat to the right temperature for the food you're cooking. On a gas grill, just twiddle the knobs. To adjust the heat on a charcoal grill, see "Charcoal Heat Control" on page 27.

USE QUICK-GRILLING FOR SMALLER, MORE TENDER FOODS. Also called direct grilling, what I call "quick-grilling" takes less than 30 minutes. This is the kind of grilling most people are used to for hamburgers, hot dogs, sausages, steaks, chops, boneless chicken breasts, fish, shellfish, vegetables, and other small or tender

Get the Right Grill

I f you're new to grilling at tailgates or only cook for a small party, you probably won't need a SuperGrillMaster3000 with all the bells and whistles. But if you're a black-belt barbecue master who regularly tackles large cuts of meat or needs to feed hordes of hungry fans, you're going to want a spacious setup with plenty of firepower. Here's how to find a grill that meets your needs:

For Newbies

If you prefer charcoal (more flavorful) over gas (more convenient), consider the "good old Weber kettle grill," suggests Russ Stevenson, a tailgate planner in Philadelphia. The standard 22-inch kettle grill offers enough space to grill over direct or indirect heat and the lid is high enough for big cuts and tall items like beer-can chicken. You can even remove the grill's legs to make it more compact during transport.

If you're traveling in a small car, you might prefer one of the many portable gas or charcoal grills now available. These smaller grills typically have folding legs (or stand less than 2 feet high) and offer cooking space from 14 to 18 inches across. Among gas portables, the Weber Q is my favorite. It's got enough grill space for 10 to 15 burgers, has a high-enough lid for a whole chicken, and weighs in at about the same size as a small family dog. Check the sources on page 182 for portable grills.

A hibachi makes another good choice for low-key grilling. About the size of a glove box, this grill has no lid. To improvise a lid, put a disposable aluminum pan upside down over the food.

For the Advanced Griller

"One thing that screams out is the Weber ranch grill. It's like a charcoal kettle grill on steroids," says grilling guru Steven Raichlen. At nearly 38 inches across, the grill offers more than 1,100 square inches of cooking area. "You can easily feed a hundred people off of it," Raichlen says. "It makes a very dramatic statement." And what is that statement? "It says, 'I am serious about my tailgating!' "

Russ Stevenson, better known as Tailgate Russ, also recommends grills such as the Freedom Grill (as seen on the cover of this book) that mount directly onto your vehicle's hitch receiver. This way you can bring a sizeable grill without having to make space in your vehicle or haul a trailer. Look for Freedom Grills and other similar hitch-mounted grills in the gear section beginning on page 182.

If you *really* want to step up to the big leagues, drop a few Benjamins on a trailer-mounted smoker pit. These huge barrel-shaped smokers allow you to stage a pig roast, smoke massive amounts of meat, and hold court like a king in a crowd of happy tailgaters.

foods. You put the food directly over the heat source (coals, gas, or wood flame) and cook it over medium-high heat.

When quick-grilling, gas grills have the advantage of instant heat control. If food starts to burn, you turn down the heat or move the food to an unheated part of the grill. On a charcoal or wood grill, use the same principle by creating two (or even three) heat zones on your grill. On one side of the grill, make a layer of hot coals as thick as your fist. That side is your medium-high-heat zone for searing meats and vegetables and quick-grilling. On the other side of the grill, spread the coals into a thinner, single layer. That's your medium-low-heat zone. Move foods over the lower heat zone if they start to burn or to finish cooking them. The low-heat zone is great for toasting bread and buns, too.

USE SLOW-GRILLING FOR BIGGER, TOUGHER FOODS. Also called indirect grilling, what I call "slow-grilling" is best for foods that will cook for more than 30 minutes. Instead of putting food directly over the heat, you keep the food away from the heat, and keep the heat medium-low or low so that the food cooks more slowly. Slow-grilling works best with foods that would otherwise burn over direct heat before being cooked all the way through. This method coaxes great flavor out of big or tough cuts of meat like beef brisket or whole tenderloin, pork shoulder or loin roasts, whole chickens and turkeys, and bone-in poultry parts.

To slow-grill on a covered kettle grill, top-loading grill, or front-loading grill, spread the coals to opposite sides and leave a large empty space in the middle. Or, put the coals on one side and leave the other side empty. I find that you get more even heating when the coals surround the food. Either way, put the food over the unheated part of the grill and close the lid. The indirect heat of the coals slowly cooks the food, kind of like slow-roasting in an oven. For fatty cuts, like brisket and pork shoulder, put a disposable aluminum drip pan under the food between the coals to catch any drips and minimize flare-ups. For foods that tend to dry out like turkey and chicken, you can even put some flavored liquid like beer, stock, wine, or citrus juice mixed with herbs or seasonings into the drip pan. The rising steam will help to keep your slow-grilled food moist while infusing it with subtle flavors.

On a flat charcoal grill or open wood-burning pit, slow-grill by raising the grill rack 2 to 3 feet above the coals. You could even raise the rack higher to slow-grill foods for a really long time, such as a whole hog on a spit that will spit-roast over the coals for a day or more.

Whenever you slow-grill with charcoal you need to add fresh coals when the old coals begin to burn out. That's about every hour or so in a typical kettle grill. If you have a chimney starter, light a new batch of coals as the others begin to die down. Pour the new hot coals right over the old ones and continue cooking. Or, if you don't have a chimney starter, put fresh unlit coals over the old hot coals and leave the lid off the grill until the new coals begin to ash over, about 10 minutes.

If your grill rack doesn't have hinged sides for adding new charcoal, just lift off the entire hot rack with well-insulated or heatproof grill gloves. Sure, you may have food on the rack. So what? Lift the whole kit and caboodle out of the grill and place it over foil on the pavement, add your fresh coals, then put the racked food back on the grill.

The technique of slow-grilling is similar on a gas grill, except you fire up some of the burners but leave the others off. If your gas grill has two burners, light one and put your food over the unlit burner. If your grill has three or more burners, fire up the outside burners and put the food over the middle unlit burners. Keep the lid down as much as possible because heat escapes every time you lift the lid, which lowers the overall temperature and lengthens cooking time.

Grilling Game Plan

Whether you use charcoal, wood, or gas, here are the basic steps—in chronological order—for perfect grilling at every tailgate. This may seem elementary, but knowing the fundamentals helps you move on to advanced grilling techniques like slow-grilling (page 25) and smoking with wood chips (page 27).

1. Light the fire.

2. Make a two-zone fire on charcoal and wood grills. (See page 25.)

3. Preheat the grill rack for at least 10 minutes.

4. Brush and oil the grill rack.

5. Grill the food and tend the fire.

6. Remove the food and let it rest a few minutes.

7. Brush the rack clean.

8. Cover the grill and turn it off or close the vents until next time.

GET SOME WOOD CHIPS. Wood chunks or wood chips are great for adding smoke flavor when slow-grilling. Whether you're cooking with charcoal or gas, think of wood chips as the spice rub on your grill's heat source. They can help turn your grill into something closer to a wood-burning barbecue pit, adding awesome barbecued flavor. Some call it barbecuing on a grill, but keep in mind that true barbecuing uses very low temperatures (225°F or less) that are difficult to maintain on a typical charcoal or gas grill.

Let's just call it smoking on a grill. Whatever you call it, wood chips are best for infusing smoke flavor into big cuts of meat that will cook slowly. These slow-grilled foods have more time to soak up the smoky aromas from the smoldering wood.

Charcoal Heat Control

If you use a charcoal grill, finding that temperature sweet spot is a little more tricky than just twisting a propane knob. To tame the flames, you manage the airflow with the grill lid and vents. Here's where a tailgater can really strut his or her stuff, instead of turning out charred hockey pucks like the neophytes.

Cover and vent. When you first spread out the hot coals, you'll have a blazing hot fire of 450°F or more. Put on the grill rack, leave off the lid, and open the vents all the way. This maximizes oxygen flow so you get the hottest fire possible. Let the rack heat up over high heat for at least 10 minutes. Then put on the grill lid and adjust the temperature as follows:

High heat: Open all the vents (top and bottom) full throttle.

Medium-high heat: Close all the vents one-quarter of the way.

Medium heat: Close all the vents halfway.

Medium-low heat: Close all the vents three-quarters of the way.

Low heat: Close all the vents all the way.

Check the temp. During cooking, check the temperature now and then and adjust the vents. Opening the vents raises the heat; closing them lowers the heat. If you have a temperature gauge or thermometer on your grill, check it to see if the temperature is right. Otherwise, lift the lid and put your hand an inch or two above the grill rack (assuming the rack itself is positioned 4 to 6 inches from the coals). Count how many seconds you can hold your hand there to find out how hot the fire is.

High heat (450° to 600°F+): 1 to 2 seconds
Medium-high heat (400° to 450°F): 3 to 4 seconds
Medium heat (350° to 400°F): 4 to 5 seconds
Medium-low heat (300° to 350°F): 5 to 6 seconds
Low heat (250°F or lower): 7+ seconds

Most tailgaters use hickory or oak chips for smoking on a grill, but different woods have different flavors. Barbecue expert Steven Raichlen recommends alder wood for salmon, chicken, and turkey; apple for chicken and pork; cherry for poultry; mesquite for beef; maple for poultry, seafood, and pork; hickory and pecan for pork; and oak for poultry, seafood, and meat in general.

SOAK THE CHIPS. To make sure the chips smoke instead of incinerate, soak them in cold water for at least 30 minutes, preferably 1 hour. The longer you soak them, the longer they'll smolder before burning up. I find it easiest to soak the chips before I leave for the tailgate so I'm ready to cook when I get there. I soak my chips on the way in a mini metal trash can with a tight-fitting lid. After the chips are gone and the grilling is done, I use the metal can to quickly dispose of the hot coals. Great for when you lose track of time at the tailgate and need to cool down the grill fast!

If you don't have a metal trash can, put the chips in a heavy-duty zipper-lock bag and fill the bag with enough cold water to cover the chips. Seal and put the bag in the cooler if you'll be soaking them on the way. Or soak them at the tailgate.

TOSS THEM ONTO THE HEAT. On a charcoal grill, you just drain the soaked chips and put a handful or two onto the hot coals. As you begin to see billows of smoke, add food to the grill. You'll have to add more chips (and more charcoal) when the first batch burns up, after about 1 hour on medium to medium-low heat. Have extra soaked chips on hand to replace the burnt ones. For the most smoke flavor, keep the grill lid down and open one of the top vents so smoke is drawn over the food on its way out the vent. If your grill doesn't have a lid, put a big disposable aluminum pan upside down over the food as a makeshift lid. It won't hold in nearly as much smoke, but it's better than nothing.

You can use wood chips on a gas grill, too. Smoking on a gas grill combines the convenience of gas with the flavor of wood smoke. Some high-end gas grills have a smoker box and dedicated burner for this purpose. If your grill has a smoker box, put a thick layer of soaked wood chips in the box. If your grill doesn't have a smoker box, use a foil cooking bag, or make a flat packet by wrapping the wood chips in foil. Poke holes in the foil packet so smoke can escape. Put the packet right over one of the hot burners. Crank the burner (or your dedicated smoker box burner) to high until you see lots of smoke, then turn the heat to whatever temperature is right for the food you're cooking.

The flavor you get from wood chips is really worth this little bit of fuss. Again, for the most smoke flavor, keep the lid down to trap the smoke.

BRUSH AND OIL THE RACK. For the best grill marks and the cleanest flavors, keep your grill rack hot, brushed, and well oiled. Scrape your preheated rack with a stiff wire grill brush. (A hot rack cleans easier than a cold rack.) Then wad up a paper towel, dip it in oil with your tongs, and wipe the oily towel over the hot rack. An oily paper towel does double duty here: it lubes up the metal bars of the rack and cleans off any remaining residue from your last grilling session. You could lube the rack with another kind of fat like a chunk of trimmed beef or pork fat. Or you could spray the rack with cooking spray (remove it from the grill to avoid flare-ups). But I find that the oily towel helps to clean the rack as well as lube it, and that means better flavor, especially if you're going to grill bananas after grilling something like a well-marbled steak.

LET FOODS OPEN UP. About 20 minutes before you start grilling, remove marinated, rubbed, or brined meats from your cooler. That gives them a chance to warm up a bit, which helps create a better crust on the surface of the meat. Rule of thumb: Warm meat sears better than cold meat. Plus, taking the meat out of the cooler early helps to warm up the interior of the meat so it can reach its cooked temperature before the outside burns to a crisp. A similar flavor principle applies to most foods. Cold food like salads, dips, and salsas hold their flavors in tight when well chilled. For the best flavor, take chilled foods out of the cooler about 15 minutes before serving.

MINIMIZE FLARE-UPS. Finally, your food is on the grill! When using the quick-grilling method, avoid flare-ups for the best flavor and least burnt taste. Flare-ups happen when fat drips onto hot coals; they tend to give grilled foods an acrid or bitter taste. To minimize flare-ups, make a two-zone fire (see page 25) or leave some empty space on your grill rack. That way you have room to move food out of any flare-up danger zones. See "Healthy Grilling" (page 30) for more ways to minimize flare-ups.

BRUSH, BASTE, AND MOP. What you put in or on your grilled food creates its signature flavor. That could be a marinade, a spice rub, a basting sauce, a mop sauce, or a finishing sauce (which goes on right at the end for flavor and sheen). For marinated foods or ones that aren't rubbed with spices, you can brush on reserved marinade or sauce by dragging the wet basting brush over the food. But for spice-rubbed foods, you don't want to scrape the seasonings off the surface of food by brushing. Here's where you baste or mop instead of brushing.

Basting is done with a brush, but instead of dragging the brush across the food, you dab it several times all over the surface so the sauce clings without disturbing whatever seasonings are already there. Mopping is usually done on bigger, tougher cuts of meat that need added moisture. Instead of using a brush, you use a barbecue mop, which looks like a kid-size version of a regular kitchen mop. You dunk the mop into your mop sauce (usually a more liquidy mixture than a barbecue sauce or finishing sauce), then let the liquid drip off the mop onto the food. If the sauce doesn't

Healthy Grilling

ome people give grilling a bad rap. They say it's all fatty meats and cite the cancer risks of grill smoke. As with any type of cooking, you can grill with health in mind or not. If health is on your mind, here are some tips for healthy grilling.

o **Make lean marinades.** Replace some of the fat in marinades with broth, yogurt, or vegetable or fruit juices like tomato juice, orange juice, or lemon juice. To boost flavor, add spice rubs or other seasoning mixes.

o **Think outside the beef.** Focus on leaner foods like pork, chicken, turkey, fish, and vegetables. Or grill a pizza or sandwich instead of a big hunk of meat. The recipes in this book offer plenty of options from grilled Spicy Steak Fries (page 59) to Grilled Stuffed French Toast (page 110).

o **Avoid flare-ups.** These happen when fat drips onto hot coals. Flare-ups make food taste like soot, but worse, the smoke can send cancer-causing molecules (called polycyclic aromatic hydrocarbons or PAHs) back to your food. According to the American Institute for Cancer Research, scientists haven't determined how much of these substances will affect you. So

they recommend erring on the side of caution. Avoid these potential carcinogens by keeping fat off the grill. Choose lean cuts of meat like top round, flank steak, tenderloin, or other loin cuts and trim away any visible fat before grilling. Cut meats into small pieces (as for kebabs) or grill them over medium-high heat so they spend less time over the coals. Or when grilling fattier cuts like beef brisket and pork shoulder, use the indirect heat of the slow-grilling method (page 25) so fat doesn't drip and cause flare-ups. Keep fat in marinades to a minimum, but definitely marinate because studies have shown that marinades can reduce another potential carcinogen called heterocyclic amines or HCAs. According to the American Institute for Cancer Research, marinades may provide a barrier that keeps the flames from touching the meat; or the citrus juice, oils, and herbs in marinades may provide some anticancer protection.

reach the entire surface of the food you can lightly dab the mop onto the food, but be careful not to loosen any dry seasonings that may already be there. You'll see this mopping method at work in the Beer-Mopped Brisket with Texas Barbecue Sauce (page 88). Look for long-handled basting brushes and barbecue mops at your hardware store or check the sources beginning on page 182.

Speaking of sauces, "don't abuse the barbecue sauce," advises grilling expert Steven Raichlen. "It should only go on at the end of cooking—or even after the food comes off the grill." Barbecue sauces are typically high in sugar, which tastes great when the sugar is lightly caramelized on the grill; but that sugar can quickly burn and ruin an otherwise good piece of food. Brush on high-sugar sauces only during the last 5 to 10 minutes, or save them for the table.

Also keep in mind that "all cooking is a relationship between time and temperature," says Cheryl Alters Jamison, co-author of *Born to Grill* and other cookbooks with husband Bill Jamison. "People cook outdoors and want to have a beer with their friends, but you need to pay attention. You can't build a blazing bonfire, throw things over it, and come back later and expect it to be all right." Moral: Tend the fire. Fortunately for some folks, tending the fire is half the fun anyway. If it's cold out, crowd around the grill and make the fire a focal point of your tailgate.

KICK YOUR GRILLING INTO HIGH GEAR. Now that you've got the techniques down, consider buying a few extra barbecue tools to grill like a pro: a grill mop for dabbing or drizzling mop sauces onto meats; a grill basket for delicate fish fillets and chopped vegetables; a rib rack for slow-grilling multiple racks of ribs at once and saving space on the grill; a vertical roaster for poultry (also a space saver); and heat-proof silicone gloves for grabbing hot meats right off the grill. "Also keep a spray bottle handy to spritz meat with apple cider vinegar or wine to add flavor and moisture," says Raichlen. "Wine works well on a rib roast turning on a spit, and cider vinegar goes well on pork butt." Be sure to pick up at least one pair of spring-loaded tongs, which are easier to use than those bent into a U-shape. Use tongs, instead of a fork, to lift up and turn meats. (Forks poke holes in the meat's crust and let flavorful juices escape into the flames, causing unnecessary flare-ups.)

If you're in the market for new grilling gear, buy it in late summer or early fall when many hardware stores discount the year's grilling inventory to make way for snow shovels.

BRANCH OUT. Get the most you can out of your grill. When the lid is off, think of the grill as an open pan and grill sandwiches, pizzas, or anything else that won't fall through the grates. When the lid is down, think of the grill as an oven and roast peppers, eggplant, potatoes, root vegetables, chestnuts, squash, or anything else you might roast in the oven. You don't just have to cook hunks of meat. "Grill a vegetable platter, mushrooms, or corn on the cob," says Jamison. "For dessert, grill apples and pears, or make grilled s'mores with chocolate, marshmallows, and graham crackers." Try new things and surprise your tailgate guests. See the recipes for grilling Black Bean Two-Cheese Quesadillas (page 61), Pesto Gorgonzola Grilled Pizza (page 62), Grilled Calzones (page 66), Grilled Stuffed French Toast (page 110), and Grilled Pound Cake and Bananas Foster (page 112).

LOCK IT DOWN. People in the Northeast ask me: "How do you keep your grill from getting stolen from the parking lot while you're at the game?" Answer: Lock it down. If you're planning to party after the game, put anything that might tempt the wayward thief back into the car, but other big items can just be locked down. Attach a cable lock (like a bike lock or other long wire lock) to your grill, your table, or your shelter and lock it to the car through one of the openings in the rim of your wheel or a strong loop under the back of your bumper. Locking down the grill comes in handy when it's still hot but you need to get into the stadium to see the game.

LEAVE YOUR AREA CLEAN. Give the stadium's cleanup crew a break. When the party's over, load your trash into bags and dump it in the nearest Dumpster. Put recyclables in a separate bag if you can. If there are no coal bins for hot coals, bring along a metal bucket with a tight-fitting lid. Dump the hot coals in the bucket and add water to douse the coals. Quickly put on the lid and, after the coals are completely cooled, dump the coals in a Dumpster. Or if you're using a small portable grill, line the bottom of the grill with heavy-duty foil or a double layer of regular foil. After the coals cool off some, put on insulated grill mitts and wrap the coals in the foil, then soak the foil bag in water until the coals are completely cooled.

If you love charcoal grilling but want to avoid the hot-coals problem at tailgates, invest in a trailer-mounted barbecue pit or Freedom Grill (as seen on the cover; see also the gear sources on page 180). Haul the grill to the parking lot with your truck, let it cool down while you're at the game, then haul it home. Simple.

IN THE
Cooler

Dips, Spreads, and Salsas

Tapenade

Basil Pesto

Spinach Artichoke Bread Bowl

Italian Tomato Relish

Simple Salsa

Black-Eyed Pea Salsa

Slaw, Salads, and Sandwiches

Creamy Slaw

Tuscan White Bean Salad

Grilled Corn Salad with Honey-Lime Dressing

Red, White, and Blue Potato Salad

Chinese Noodle Salad

Pesto Tortellini Salad

Gridiron Grinder

Sweets and Desserts

Buckeye Candy

Chocolate Whiskey Pudding

Piña Colada Cake

Tapenade

Don't let the name throw you. Tapenade (ta-pen-AHD) is a kind of Mediterranean relish made from olives and capers. It has a bitingly fresh and rich flavor that perks up just about anything. I like to spread it on crackers or slather it over grilled tuna steaks, pork tenderloin, or lamb chops. Try it on Bruschetta (page 60). It goes almost anywhere—snack, dip, topping for main dish. Tapenade is a good basic spread to have at a tailgate. The proportions here make over 3 cups but it keeps in the fridge for a month or two. Halve the recipe if you want less. Don't use canned olives—they have a metallic taste. **MAKES ABOUT 3½ CUPS**

2 cups pitted black olives, preferably oil-cured, niçoise, or kalamata

¼ cup drained capers

1 can (2 ounces) anchovies, rinsed and patted dry

2 garlic cloves, chopped

¼ cup extra virgin olive oil

Juice of ½ lemon

1 tablespoon fresh thyme

3 cups loosely packed fresh parsley

½ teaspoon ground black pepper

BEFORE YOU GO: Put everything in a food processor and blend until finely minced but not completely pureed, about 20 seconds. Spoon into a serving bowl or zipper-lock bag, cover or seal, and chill in refrigerator or cooler.

WHEN YOU GET THERE: Remove from cooler 20 minutes before serving or using.

NEIGHBORLY TIP If you don't like anchovies, replace them with 1½ cups pine nuts.

Basil Pesto

Here's another all-purpose spread, topping, and sauce. Spoon it over grilled salmon. Make it the sauce for pizza, or use it as a sandwich spread. Sure, you could buy the jarred stuff, but homemade is so much better. Pesto takes less than 5 minutes to make and it keeps frozen for months. I make it in August or September when fresh basil is easy to find. Then I just freeze it in a tub and scoop out whatever I need.

MAKES ABOUT 2¼ CUPS

2 large garlic cloves, coarsely chopped

10 cups loosely packed fresh basil

2 cups grated imported Parmigiano-Reggiano cheese

¾ cup pine nuts

1 teaspoon salt

¼ teaspoon ground black pepper

1 cup extra virgin olive oil

BEFORE YOU GO: Put everything but oil in a food processor. Blend until finely chopped, about 30 seconds. Scrape down sides of processor bowl, then add ¾ cup of the oil and blend to a loose paste, about 20 seconds, scraping bowl as necessary. For a more runny pesto, blend in remaining oil a tablespoon at a time until thinned how you like it. Scrape into two small airtight containers and chill up to 1 week or freeze up to 1 year. Two containers allow you to carry just 1 cup of pesto at a time, since you'll rarely need 2 cups.

WHEN YOU GET THERE: If the pesto is frozen, use a melon baller or spoon to scrape out the amount you need; small pieces will melt quickly when they meet hot foods. Or thaw and remove from cooler 20 minutes before using as a spread or dip.

NEIGHBORLY TIP If you'll only use a small amount of pesto at a time, drop the prepared pesto in 1-tablespoon blobs onto wax-paper-lined cookie sheets. Freeze until solid, then pop off the blobs and seal in a zipper-lock bag. That way you have 1-tablespoon amounts ready to go.

Spinach Artichoke Bread Bowl

Versions of this warm dip have become standard bar food around the country. And, to me, tailgating is like being at an outdoor bar. Here's some bar food for the party— served in a bread bowl. All the prep is done at home, then you just reheat the dip onsite. **MAKES 12 SERVINGS**

1 tablespoon olive oil

½ cup finely chopped red onion

1 large garlic clove, minced

½ cup mayonnaise

1 container (8 ounces) sour cream, about 1 cup

1 jar (6 ounces) marinated artichoke hearts, drained and finely chopped

1 package (10 ounces) frozen chopped spinach, thawed and squeezed dry

¾ cup grated Parmesan cheese

¼ teaspoon salt

¼ teaspoon paprika

2 small round or oblong loaves pumpernickel or sourdough bread (about 1 pound each)

BEFORE YOU GO: Warm oil in medium saucepan over medium heat. When hot, add onion and garlic. Cook until soft, about 5 minutes. Reduce heat to medium-low and stir in remaining ingredients, except bread. Cook until heated through. Cover and chill in refrigerator or cooler up to 2 days.

The morning of the tailgate, cut one loaf of bread into 1-inch cubes and put in zipper-lock bag. Make a bread bowl with other loaf: Cut out top of loaf as if making a jack-o'-lantern out of a pumpkin. Remove bread from inside, leaving 1-inch shell of crust. Cut removed bread into 1-inch cubes, add to zipper-lock bag, and seal. Seal bread bowl in another zipper-lock bag.

WHEN YOU GET THERE: Reheat dip over medium-low heat, stirring now and then, until hot, 5 to 8 minutes. Scrape dip into bread bowl and serve with bread cubes.

NEIGHBORLY TIPS Keep the dip warm a little longer by heating the bread bowl. Wrap bread bowl in heavy-duty foil and put on a medium-low covered grill until warm and just crisp on the crust, about 5 minutes per side. Unwrap and fill with the warm dip.

If you're watching calories, use low-fat mayo and sour cream. But, remember, fat is a tailgater's friend. It helps to keep you warm on those chilly December days.

Super-Duper Bowl

Cooking for a crowd sometimes means going to extremes. Super-big grills, big steaks . . . even big bowls of dip. To celebrate the 2004 U.S. college football season finale, the Extreme Team at Friendship Dairies mixed a colossal bowl of dip weighing 2,314 pounds—enough for 32,000 hungry tailgaters!

This appetizer easily became the world's biggest dip, beating the previous Guinness world-record holder, an 1,807-pound bowl of guacamole made in Australia in 1999. The new champion was served up salsa style, including sour cream, tomatoes, onions, bell peppers, jalapeño chiles, and fresh cilantro.

Italian Tomato Relish

Commercial versions of this relish often go by the name of "bruschetta." That's actually a misnomer but understandable because the relish is found so often on top of the grilled bread called Bruschetta (page 60). Try the relish also on sandwiches, over grilled beef or chicken, or as a dip for crackers. **MAKES ABOUT 1½ CUPS**

¼ cup finely chopped sweet onion, such as Vidalia

2 ripe medium tomatoes, seeded and finely chopped

2 garlic cloves, minced

2 tablespoons chopped basil or 1 tablespoon dried

3 tablespoons olive oil

⅛ teaspoon salt

Pinch of ground black pepper

BEFORE YOU GO: Rinse chopped onion in colander or your hands under cold water, then put in medium serving bowl or small zipper-lock bag. Mix in remaining ingredients. Cover and chill in refrigerator or cooler. Keeps about 1 week.

WHEN YOU GET THERE: Remove from cooler 20 minutes before serving.

NEIGHBORLY TIP Rinsing the onion helps to mellow its raw bite.

Simple Salsa

*What's a party without salsa and chips? This basic tomato salsa blows away any-
thing you'll get in a jar. And you can put it together right before you leave for the
tailgate. For extra hot salsa, leave the seeds in the jalapeño peppers.*

MAKES ABOUT 4 CUPS

4 ripe medium tomatoes, seeded and finely chopped

5 jalapeño chiles, seeded and finely chopped

1 large garlic clove, minced

½ cup finely chopped red onion

½ cup chopped fresh cilantro

Juice of 2 small limes

1 teaspoon salt

BEFORE YOU GO: The morning of the tailgate, mix all ingredients in bowl with lid or
in large zipper-lock bag. Seal and chill in refrigerator or cooler.

WHEN YOU GET THERE: Remove from cooler 20 minutes before serving.

NEIGHBORLY TIPS If you're time crunched, look for fresh salsa sold in tubs in the
refrigerated produce section of your grocery store. Refrigerated salsa usually
tastes better than jarred salsa.

Serve with Mexican-flavored steaks and other meats.

For Simple Grilled Salsa, grill the whole tomatoes, whole jalapeños, and unpeeled
garlic over medium heat until blackened all over. Skewer the garlic so it's easier to
handle. The tomatoes and chiles will take 3 to 5 minutes per side; the garlic will
take a little longer and will only blacken in spots. The flavor of garlic mellows on
the grill, so consider using double the amount. Take the veggies off the grill and let
cool. Peel the tomatoes and garlic, then finely chop them. Finely chop the chiles.
Mix everything in a bowl with the remaining ingredients. This salsa will be hotter
because the seeds are left in the chiles. For a milder salsa, use fewer chiles. If you
have time and grill space, you can make this version at the tailgate.

Black-Eyed Pea Salsa

My friend Kevin Ireland lives in Gainesville, Florida, home of the Florida Gators. One year, I took a road trip with a few buddies to stay with Kevin and go to a Gators-Razorbacks matchup. Kevin's wife, Susan, brought this salsa to the tailgate, but I was so busy grilling up steaks and chops, it was gone before I could sample it. Susan generously gave me the recipe and I tried it after I got home. Ooo-eee, is it good. And so easy. Break out the tortilla chips! Tastes great with bagel chips, too. **MAKES 8 SERVINGS**

¼ cup balsamic vinegar

3 tablespoons sugar

⅓ cup olive oil

1 teaspoon salt

2 cans (15 ounces each) black-eyed peas, rinsed and drained

4 scallions (green and white parts), thinly sliced

4 ripe medium tomatoes, seeded and finely chopped

2 large garlic cloves, minced

¼ cup chopped fresh cilantro

2 California red (Fresno) or red jalapeño chiles, seeded and chopped

BEFORE YOU GO: Whisk together vinegar, sugar, oil, and salt in medium bowl until blended, 2 to 3 minutes. Stir in everything else. Cover and chill in refrigerator or cooler at least 1 hour or up to 1 day.

WHEN YOU GET THERE: Remove from cooler 20 minutes before serving.

NEIGHBORLY TIP True to the South, this salsa is on the sweet side. You could cut the sugar to 1 or 2 tablespoons, if you like.

SLAW, SALADS, AND SANDWICHES

Creamy Slaw

Barbecues are almost unthinkable without coleslaw. Too often, though, the slaw is drowning in gobs of lifeless, gluey mayonnaise. I like a bit more attitude in my slaw. This one mixes mayonnaise and sour cream for sharper flavor and dilutes the creamy texture with a couple shots of puckery vinegar. Sugar and salt balance out the flavors. **MAKES 8 SERVINGS**

¼ cup cider vinegar

2 tablespoons mayonnaise

2 tablespoons sour cream

2 tablespoons sugar

1 teaspoon salt

¼ teaspoon ground black pepper

1 package (1 pound) coleslaw mix (grated cabbage and carrots)

BEFORE YOU GO: The morning of the tailgate, mix together everything but the coleslaw mix in large bowl with fork or whisk until blended. Stir in coleslaw mix. Cover and chill in refrigerator or cooler up to 6 hours.

WHEN YOU GET THERE: Enjoy as a side dish with Beer-Mopped Brisket with Texas Barbecue Sauce (page 88) or on sandwiches like Carolina Pulled Pork (page 77).

NEIGHBORLY TIP Coleslaw mix is available in the bagged salad section of most grocery stores. Fresh cabbage and carrots are even better if you have time to shred them. You'll need half of 1 medium head green cabbage and 1 large carrot, both shredded with a food processor shredding disk or by hand with a knife.

Tuscan White Bean Salad

Here's a quick bean salad that everyone seems to love. Red wine vinegar gives it head-turning zip and fresh rosemary lends a deeply refreshing, pinelike aroma.

MAKES 8 SIDE-DISH SERVINGS

RED WINE VINAIGRETTE

¼ cup good-quality red wine vinegar

½ cup extra virgin olive oil

1 garlic clove, crushed

½ teaspoon salt

¼ teaspoon ground black pepper

SALAD

1 red bell pepper, finely chopped

1 medium cucumber, peeled, seeded, and finely chopped

16 grape tomatoes, quartered

3⅓ cups cooked or canned Great Northern beans, rinsed and drained

2 tablespoons chopped fresh rosemary

BEFORE YOU GO: Put vinegar in medium bowl with tight-fitting lid. Whisk in oil in a slow steady stream, until fully blended, about 1 minute. Whisk in garlic, salt, and pepper. Stir in salad ingredients, cover, and chill in refrigerator or cooler up to 2 days.

WHEN YOU GET THERE: Remove from cooler 20 minutes before serving.

Grilled Corn Salad with Honey-Lime Dressing

I made this salad for the 2002 U.S. World Cup quarterfinals between the U.S. and Mexico. The Mexican flavor is there in the corn and lime, but in the end, American tastes win over with the cucumber and mint. And that's how the game played out when the U.S. upset Mexico 2-0. Try this salad at any warm-weather tailgate.

MAKES 6 SERVINGS

5 ears Grilled Corn on the Cob (page 58)

Juice of 1 lime

¼ cup olive oil

2 teaspoons honey

½ teaspoon salt

⅛ teaspoon ground black pepper

½ cup finely chopped red onion

1 small cucumber, finely chopped

½ red bell pepper, finely chopped

1 tablespoon chopped fresh mint

BEFORE YOU GO (or when you get there if you'll be grilling): Grill corn as directed, omitting butter, salt, and pepper. Cool enough to handle, then stand corncobs upright on cutting board with fat end down. Cut straight down, slicing kernels off cobs.

Put lime juice in medium bowl, then gradually whisk in oil in a slow, steady stream until fully incorporated. Whisk in honey, salt, and pepper. Stir in corn, onion, cucumber, bell pepper, and mint, breaking up strips of corn. Serve immediately or chill in refrigerator or cooler up to 3 days.

NEIGHBORLY TIP If you can't grill the corn, remove the husks and silks and cook it in a large pot of boiling water with 1 tablespoon sugar. Cover, return to a boil, and boil for 3 minutes. Remove from heat and let stand, covered, 5 minutes. Use as directed in recipe.

Red, White, and Blue Potato Salad

This isn't your classic potato salad, heavy on the mayo and mashed egg. You can buy that in any store. This one has a lighter dressing to show off the colors of the spuds—with just a little mayo and sour cream for richness and flavor. I steam the potatoes to help keep the colors bright (why let them boil away into the water?). Choose the colors based on your team colors: red, white, and blue; red and blue; red and white; or blue and white. Pick up some spuds that are colored all the way through the flesh, not just on the skin. Farmers' markets usually carry these kinds of potatoes. If you can't find them, use the ones with colored skins from your grocery store.

MAKES 8 TO 10 SERVINGS

3 pounds small red, white, and blue potatoes, scrubbed, skins left on

3 tablespoons extra virgin olive oil

2 tablespoons white wine vinegar

2 tablespoons chopped fresh parsley

1 tablespoon sour cream

1 tablespoon mayonnaise

1 tablespoon Dijon mustard

1 scallion (green and white parts), chopped

1 teaspoon salt

½ teaspoon ground black pepper

½ teaspoon celery seed, optional

BEFORE YOU GO: Cut spuds into 1-inch chunks and put in steamer basket set over pan of simmering water. Cover and steam over medium heat until potatoes are fork tender, 10 to 12 minutes. Let cool a few minutes.

Mix everything else in large bowl. Add warm potatoes and mix. Let cool, cover, and chill in refrigerator or cooler up to 4 hours.

WHEN YOU GET THERE: Remove from cooler 20 minutes before serving and serve within 2 hours.

NEIGHBORLY TIPS For a little pig in your salad, cook 3 slices bacon until crisp, then crumble and mix into the salad.

To fancify the flavor, replace the parsley with 1 tablespoon chopped fresh tarragon and/or dill.

This salad is best warm. To serve it that way at the tailgate, toss the salad into a disposable aluminum pan and put it on your grill over medium-low heat until the spuds are just warmed up.

If you don't have a steamer insert for your pan, the recipe works fine when you boil the spuds, although they may lose a bit of color.

By the Numbers

Sports are all about numbers. Most RBIs, best running average, fastest lap . . . and on and on. Here are some numbers you don't always hear about.

- Largest sporting venue in the world: Indianapolis Motor Speedway (capacity 250,000)

- Number of bricks that formerly paved the speedway, giving it the nickname "Brickyard": 3.2 million

- Highest attendance at a Super Bowl: 103,985 at Super Bowl XIV (Steelers vs. Rams)

- Highest score in a regular season NFL game: Redskins (72) vs. Giants (41).

- First intercollegiate football game: Rutgers vs. Princeton, Nov. 6, 1869. Rutgers won.

- Nation's loudest stadium (according to *The Sporting News*): University of Florida's Florida Field, also known as "The Swamp"

- Coldest game in NFL history: Many sources, including the Packers, claim it was the Dec. 31, 1967, "Ice Bowl" at Green Bay vs. Dallas with a kickoff temperature of −13°F and a −48°F wind chill. According to the NFL, however, the coldest game on record was January 10, 1982, Cincinnati vs. San Diego, with a kickoff temperature of −9°F and a wind chill of −59°F.

- First year in which a player was paid to play football: 1892. William Heffelfinger was paid $500 by the Allegheny Athletic Association to play against the Pittsburgh Athletic Club. The investment paid off: they won.

- First televised NFL game: 1939, Brooklyn vs. Philadelphia

Chinese Noodle Salad

My son, August, always asks for cold peanut noodles. It's the peanut butter he's really after. I haven't met a kid yet who doesn't love peanut butter. Even kids allergic to peanuts seem to crave it. How could you not love anything with "butter" in its name? Except maybe ball handlers nicknamed Butterfingers. Creamy peanut butter is the key flavor in this salad, which is similar to the cold sesame noodles you get at Chinese takeout joints. This version has a few more layers of flavor with fresh ginger, slivered snow peas, and fresh cilantro. My kids dig it at games. **MAKES 8 SERVINGS**

1 pound dried Chinese wheat noodles or linguine

1 cup snow peas, about ¼ pound

1 cup hot vegetable broth or chicken broth

1 tablespoon brown sugar

1 cup creamy peanut butter

1 tablespoon grated fresh ginger

½ cup tamari or soy sauce

¼ cup unsweetened rice vinegar

1 tablespoon toasted sesame oil

1 teaspoon hot pepper sauce

2 tablespoons chopped fresh cilantro

2 teaspoons sesame seeds

BEFORE YOU GO: Up to 2 days before, cook noodles according to package directions until tender but not mushy.

Slice snow peas lengthwise into thin strips.

Mix broth and sugar in large bowl until sugar melts. Whisk in peanut butter, ginger, tamari or soy sauce, rice vinegar, sesame oil, hot pepper sauce, and cilantro.

Just before draining noodles, transfer 3 tablespoons hot noodle water to bowl and mix it in. Drain noodles and run under cold water to stop the cooking. Add noodles to bowl along with snow peas. Mix thoroughly and scatter sesame seeds over top. Cover and chill in refrigerator or cooler up to 2 days.

WHEN YOU GET THERE: Remove from cooler 20 minutes before serving to open up the flavors.

Tailgating History: The Highlight Reel

America's favorite parking-lot pastime is a curious blend of beer, barbecue, and spectator sports. Here are highlights from more than two centuries of evolution.

1861. Manassas, Virginia. At the Civil War's Battle of Bull Run, spectators line up to watch the event, carting in pies and other edibles.

1893. Princeton, New Jersey. First National Championship football game is held on Thanksgiving Day (Princeton vs. Yale). Fifty thousand spectators attend, some of whom rent carriages and eat picnic lunches on the roof.

1922. College Station, Texas. At A&M University, E. King Gill begins the tailgating tradition of football spectators acting as the "Twelfth Man" on the field, supporting and serving the team.

1927. Dearborn, Michigan. Ford releases the Model A Station Wagon, the first automobile with a fold-down tailgate.

1952. Palatine, Illinois. Weber markets the kettle grill, which becomes the standard charcoal grill in America.

2002. San Antonio, Texas. The American Tailgating Association (ATA) emerges as the country's largest tailgating club. The ATA estimates that between 20 and 23 million people tailgate annually in the United States.

2003. North Hills, California. Galpin Motors releases the first-ever Tailgate Party Truck, a Ford pickup complete with built-in grill, two refrigerated beer kegs, flip-down DVD player, custom stereo, sink, ice chest, and blender, all in the truck's bed.

Pesto Tortellini Salad

Put this pasta salad out while your main dish is on the grill. It's a good staple food to fill up the fans for a long day of cheering. The dominant colors here are green and white—perfect for a New York Jets tailgate. If you're a Jets purist, leave out the red tomato. **MAKES 8 SERVINGS**

2 pounds refrigerated or frozen cheese tortellini

½ cup frozen peas

½ cup Basil Pesto (page 35) or prepared pesto

2 tablespoons extra virgin olive oil

1 tomato, seeded and chopped

2 chopped scallions (green and white parts) or ¼ cup chopped onion

½ teaspoon salt

¼ teaspoon ground black pepper

BEFORE YOU GO: Cook tortellini in pot of boiling salted water according to package directions. Add peas during last 2 minutes of cooking. Drain pasta and peas together. Let cool slightly.

Mix pesto and olive oil in large bowl. Stir in tomato, scallions, salt, pepper, pasta, and peas. Cover and chill in refrigerator or cooler up to 2 days.

WHEN YOU GET THERE: Remove from cooler 20 minutes before serving.

Gridiron Grinder

Hero, hoagie, grinder, submarine, po' boy … it seems every region of the U.S.A. has its own name for a sandwich served on a long roll. Here's a classic Italian combination that's perfect for a big table spread. You can assemble it ahead so all you have to do when you get there is slice and serve. Be sure to use good-quality bread. A hero is only as good as its ingredients. **MAKES 8 SERVINGS**

2 loaves Italian or French bread (each about 1 pound)

½ cup Red Wine Vinaigrette (page 42) or your favorite salad dressing

12 ounces sliced provolone cheese

1 pound thinly sliced smoked ham

12 ounces thinly sliced Genoa salami

12 ounces thinly sliced prosciutto, preferably Parma

1 jar (12 ounces) roasted red peppers, drained

2 cups shredded lettuce

2 tomatoes, thinly sliced

1 teaspoon dried oregano

BEFORE YOU GO: The morning of the tailgate, slice bread lengthwise and open up like a book. Brush bottom halves of bread with vinaigrette. Layer half of the provolone over bottom half of both sandwiches. Layer on the ham, salami, prosciutto, roasted peppers, lettuce, tomatoes, and oregano (fold the sliced meats to build volume into the sandwich). Top with other half of provolone. Put on bread tops and wrap in wax paper, foil, or plastic. Chill in refrigerator or cooler. Bring along remaining vinaigrette.

WHEN YOU GET THERE: Remove sandwiches from cooler 20 minutes before serving. Open tops of sandwiches, lift up cheese, and drizzle remaining vinaigrette over each sandwich. Put cheese and tops back on, slice on a diagonal, and serve.

NEIGHBORLY TIP To save time, pick up everything already prepared at the supermarket: shredded lettuce and sliced tomatoes from the salad bar, sliced meats and cheeses from the deli counter, bread from the bakery, roasted peppers from the Italian section, and even bottled red wine vinaigrette.

Buckeye Candy

I met Becky Barker over the Internet. Becky writes romance novels and went to college at Ohio State University, where buckeyes are a passion. OSU's football team is called the Buckeyes; Brutus Buckeye is the official mascot; and buckeye candy is Ohio's almost official state confection. Becky generously shared her recipe for buckeye candy, which tastes exactly like a Reese's peanut butter cup. But the look is all buckeye: round and dark brown with a tan center. These candies are reminiscent of both a male deer's eye and the Ohio buckeye nut, which is named after the deer. Nomenclature aside, these chocolate-covered peanut butter balls don't last long, so make the full recipe. Clear out a little freezer or fridge space so they can chill. Becky uses a mix of semisweet and milk chocolate in her buckeyes, but I like pure bittersweet chocolate. Choose whatever chocolate you like best. **MAKES ABOUT 60 BUCKEYES**

12 tablespoons (1½ sticks) unsalted butter

4 cups confectioners' sugar

1 jar (18 ounces) creamy peanut butter, about 2 cups

1 teaspoon vanilla extract

½ teaspoon salt

12 ounces semisweet or bittersweet chocolate (chips or broken-up bar)

1 teaspoon vegetable shortening

BEFORE YOU GO: Up to 1 week before, cut butter into pieces and put in a largish microwave-safe bowl. Microwave on high until just melted, about 1 minute. Mix in sugar, peanut butter, vanilla, and salt until blended. Roll into 1-inch balls between your palms and put in single layer on large cookie sheets lined with wax paper or coated with cooking spray. Chill until firm, about 20 minutes in freezer or 2 hours in refrigerator.

Put chocolate and vegetable shortening in medium microwave-safe bowl (make sure bowl is completely dry to prevent chocolate from seizing up). Microwave on medium in 1-minute increments until chocolate is just melted enough to stir smooth, about 3 minutes total. Stop and stir every minute to avoid overcooking.

Insert a toothpick into center of a firm peanut butter ball and dip partway into melted chocolate, leaving about a ½-inch "eye" of peanut butter visible at top. Spin toothpick to release excess chocolate, then return coated ball to cookie sheet and slide out toothpick. Repeat with remaining balls and chocolate, remelting chocolate and refreezing balls as necessary. (If you're good with your hands, use both hands and dip two balls at once.)

Chill until firm, about 30 minutes in freezer or 2 hours in refrigerator. Use a knife tip to smooth tops and cover toothpick holes. Transfer to airtight container (between layers of wax paper if necessary) and chill up to 1 week in refrigerator or cooler or up to 1 month in freezer.

WHEN YOU GET THERE: Serve chilled.

NEIGHBORLY TIPS For a creamier-tasting, less chocolatey coating, use 6 ounces milk chocolate and 6 ounces semisweet chocolate. For a more pure chocolate hit, use 12 ounces bittersweet chocolate. For the middle ground, use all semisweet chocolate.

If you have kids, get them to help dip the buckeyes. That could speed things up considerably, depending on your kids.

Chocolate Whiskey Pudding

Ahh … chocolate and whiskey: two of my favorite flavors. Use whatever whiskey you have on hand: blended or straight, from Kentucky, Tennessee, Ireland, or Scotland. A quarter cup gives the pudding a gentle whiskey flavor. Use up to a half cup if you have devout whiskey drinkers in the crowd. **MAKES 6 SERVINGS**

¾ cup sugar

3 tablespoons cornstarch

3 large eggs

¼ cup whiskey

1 cup half-and-half

1½ cups whole milk

3 ounces (3 squares) unsweetened chocolate, chopped

2 tablespoons unsalted butter

1½ teaspoons vanilla extract

Whipped cream, optional

BEFORE YOU GO: Whisk together sugar and cornstarch in medium saucepan. Whisk in eggs, then put pan over medium heat. Whisk in whiskey, half-and-half, and milk, whisking constantly until lumps disappear and mixture begins to thicken, 10 to 12 minutes. Keep just below a simmer. Whisk in chocolate until melted. Remove from heat and whisk in butter and vanilla. (Yes, a whisk is the best tool here. It ain't called whiskey pudding for nuthin'! If you don't have one, use a fork and stir vigorously.)

Pour pudding into one large or several small bowls. Cover with plastic wrap, pressing wrap directly onto pudding to prevent a skin from forming. Chill in refrigerator until cold for up to 1 day. Transfer to cooler.

WHEN YOU GET THERE: Serve in bowls with whipped cream, if using.

NEIGHBORLY TIPS Some folks like the combination of chocolate and chile peppers. And I'm one of them. If you like sweet heat, stir ½ teaspoon cayenne into the pudding along with the sugar.

Double the recipe for a big crowd. Trust me, it'll get eaten.

If you're a do-it-yourselfer, make whipped cream in your team's colors at the game. Fresh whipped cream takes only 5 minutes to make and blows away the canned stuff and whipped topping. Put a whisk or beaters in a medium glass bowl and stash it in the coldest part of your cooler. Put a half pint of heavy cream and some food coloring there, too. (The idea is to keep everything as cold as possible.) When you're ready for dessert, pour the cream into the bowl and whisk or beat at medium speed until the cream forms soft peaks when the whisk or beaters are lifted. Whisk or beat in 8 to 10 drops food coloring, 2 teaspoons vanilla extract, and 2 tablespoons granulated sugar, confectioners' sugar, or corn syrup (these last two help to stabilize the cream better than granulated sugar). Dollop over your dessert and enjoy.

Packer-Supporting Company Cuts All Kinds of Cheese

Love 'em or hate 'em, you have to admit: those foam cheesehead hats on Green Bay Packers fans make a unique fashion statement. Here's a little trivia about the Wisconsin chapeau.

- According to newspaper accounts, cheesehead inventor Ralph Bruno was struck with a flash of inspiration in 1987 when he removed a foam cushion from his mother's couch, which was being reupholstered. He cut it into a cheese-shaped wedge, spray-painted it, and stuck it on his head. The hat world was never the same.

- In 1995, as the single-engine Cessna airplane he was riding in tumbled toward the ground, Frank Emmert covered his face with his cheesehead hat. Though badly banged up, Frank made it through the crash without head trauma, attesting to the power of cheeseheads.

- The company that makes the cheeseheads, Foamation, Inc., also makes headwear in the shape of a cheese-colored top hat and fire helmet. For the true fan, the company offers cheese-shaped neckties, car-antenna toppers, rearview-mirror dice, and drink coasters.

Piña Colada Cake

Several years ago when I was working on a weight-loss cookbook, Judy Temple shared her recipe for pineapple cake. I thought the cake would be great with a little more fat and flavor. I've tinkered with the cake many times, changing the flavors each time, all with decent results. Here is the tailgate version: a yellow cake doused with rum and pineapple, then slathered with coconut pudding and crowned with whipped topping. It's the kind of easy cake you can put together the night before, toss into the cooler in the morning, then pull out at the tailgate for dessert. The dominant colors are orange and white, perfect for the Orange Bowl. Garnish with mint if you want some green. **MAKES 12 SERVINGS**

1 package (18 ounces) yellow cake mix

3 large eggs

$\frac{2}{3}$ cup rum (light, dark, or a mix)

8 tablespoons (1 stick) unsalted butter, softened

1 can (20 ounces) crushed pineapple in juice

8 ounces cream cheese

2 cups half-and-half

1 package (3.4 ounces) instant cream of coconut–flavored pudding and pie filling

$\frac{1}{8}$ teaspoon cinnamon

$\frac{1}{8}$ teaspoon nutmeg

1 container (8 ounces) whipped topping, thawed if frozen

1 can (15 ounces) mandarin oranges, drained, optional

BEFORE YOU GO: The night before, heat oven to 325°F or according to cake mix package directions. Grease a 13 × 9–inch pan with butter or cooking spray.

Make cake mix batter according to package directions, using eggs, rum, and butter. Pour into pan and bake according to package directions. Cool completely in pan on a rack. Poke holes all over cake with pinky or handle of small wooden spoon (you need largish holes to accommodate the pineapple bits). Pour pineapple and juice evenly over cake and into holes.

In large bowl, using electric mixer, beat cream cheese until smooth. Add half-and-half, pudding mix, cinnamon, and nutmeg. Beat 3 minutes then let set slightly. Spoon over pineapple, spreading evenly. Spread with whipped topping, cover tightly, and chill in refrigerator or cooler.

WHEN YOU GET THERE: Uncover and arrange oranges on top, if using.

Go Easy on the Cleanup Crew

Remember what your college apartment looked like the morning after a party? Now imagine having sixty-five thousand or so people trashing the place, and you get a sense of the cleanup involved after an NFL tailgating fest.

An Associated Press story from 2003 offered a look into the lives of the cleanup crews who shovel away the debris left in parking lots around Heinz Field after Pittsburgh Steelers games. The cleaning company responsible for the job removes up to twenty tons of trash after a game, sometimes laboring until dawn to get the lots open to daily commuters who park there. They find plenty of beer bottles and picnic coolers, which is no surprise. But they also cart away cast-off underwear. And pig heads.

Fortunately, the cleanup crew sometimes finds cool stuff left behind by careless revelers, like stereos, lawn chairs, and heaters. Still, considering they also have to pick up buckets used as latrines, a stereo would have to be pretty nice to serve as a perk for cleaning up this sort of mess. Remember: if you bring it to the party, take it home afterward. Or at least put it in a trash can.

Three Reasons to Stay Seated

Your reasons for leaving the game early sounded good the night before: your kid was cranky; you were tired after a long week; and you wanted to beat the traffic out of the stadium. Anyway, your team was getting creamed. Why stay?

Now all you can do is kick yourself, since your home boys decided to earn their paychecks and finally rallied. And you missed it. Here are a few memorable last-minute routs.

o The Giants and Eagles have been stealing wins from each other since 1978. That's the year this long-running rivalry got really bitter with the infamous fumble by Joe Pisarcik. The Giants were ahead and running out the final seconds on the clock when Pisarcik handed off to Larry Csonka. The ball got loose and the Eagles' Herman Edwards picked it up. Edwards ran in the ball and gave Philadelphia a 19–17 win.

o The third quarter had arrived on Jan. 3, 1993, to find the Oilers destroying the Bills 35–3. Buffalo rallied in the NFL's all-time biggest comeback and handed the Oilers a 41–38 defeat in overtime.

o The Jets were getting creamed by the Dolphins 30–7 on Oct. 23, 2000. But in a fourth-quarter flurry of action, the Jets pulled ahead and squeaked out a victory with a score of 40–37.

o Plenty of Colts fans were hanging their heads on Oct. 6, 2003, convinced the Buccaneers were going to send their team home in shame. After all, with four minutes left in regulation and a score of 35–14, how could the Bucs lose? Well, they did. The Colts became the "first team in NFL history to win after trailing by 21 or more points with less than four minutes to play in regulation," according to ESPN.

ON THE Grill

Starters and Sides

Grilled Corn on the Cob

Spicy Steak Fries

Bruschetta

Pizza and Sandwiches

Black Bean Two-Cheese Quesadillas

Pesto Gorgonzola Grilled Pizza

Chicken Pesto Panini

Grilled Calzones

Brats in Beer

Pork, Beef, and Buffalo

Rum-Cardamom Pork Chops

Smoky Rubbed Ribs

Chipotle-Bourbon Ribs

Carolina Pulled Pork

Buffalo Burgers

Buffalo Fajitas

Beer and Coffee Steaks

Tequila Tri-Tip

Beer-Mopped Brisket with Texas Barbecue Sauce

Chicken

Buffalo Chicken Wings

Chicken Spiedies

Barbecued Chicken

Jerk Chicken

Beer-Butt Chicken

Seafood

Chipotle-Lime Shrimp with Grilled Salsa

Beer Boiled Shrimp

Maple-Rosemary Planked Salmon

Swordfish Steaks with Pineapple Relish

Miami Dolphinfish Steaks

Breakfast and Dessert

Grilled Stuffed French Toast

Grilled Pound Cake and Bananas Foster

Grilled Corn on the Cob

There are lots of ways to grill corn: husks removed and cobs slathered with oil; in the husks with silks removed; wrapped in foil right in the coals; or right on the grill, husk and all. This last method is my favorite for tailgating. It's the easiest. Plus, it's one of the few times you can totally incinerate the surface of your food yet still get some good eats. That means you don't have to watch the grill too carefully and can relax into the tailgate. **MAKES 8 EARS (THAT'S 4 SERVINGS FOR ME; BUT I REALLY LIKE CORN)**

> 8 ears fresh corn, in the husk
>
> 3 tablespoons butter
>
> Salt, in a shaker
>
> Ground pepper, in a shaker, optional

BEFORE YOU GO: Keep corn as cold as possible until grilling.

WHEN YOU GET THERE: Heat grill to medium-high and let rack get good and hot. Grill whole ears of corn on rack until charred all over, about 15 minutes, turning now and then. The ends of the silks will burn up. If you want to be all neat about it, cut them off before grilling. Let cool enough to handle, then peel back the husks; the silks should come off right along with the husk. Roll the corn in the butter or vice versa. Sprinkle with salt and pepper, if using.

NEIGHBORLY TIPS The sugars in corn begin converting to starch as soon as the ears are cut off the stalks. That means the older your corn is, the less sweet and more starchy it will taste. For the sweetest, most crisp-tasting corn, keep it packed on ice until just before cooking.

If you want dark-roasted kernels, peel back the husks and silks before grilling, oil up the cobs, and grill the cobs on the rack until the kernels are tender and browned all over, about 10 minutes, turning often.

Instead of butter, try slathering the corn with Basil Pesto (page 35), Tapenade (page 34), or Jerk Paste (page 96). Or shake on other seasonings besides salt and pepper: try paprika, cayenne or chipotle powder, or Old Bay seasoning.

Spicy Steak Fries

Here's the perfect accompaniment for grilled steak or chicken. The prep takes less than 5 minutes, so I make this whole recipe at the tailgate. If you want to get a jump on things, you could marinate the potatoes before you go. Just keep in mind that, in transit, the butter will solidify in the bag. No problem. Just pluck out the potato pieces with tongs and grill them. The butter will re-melt when the potatoes hit the grill. **MAKES 4 SERVINGS**

4 large Yukon Gold or other yellow-fleshed potatoes, scrubbed

4 tablespoons (½ stick) butter, melted

1 teaspoon paprika

1 teaspoon salt

¼ teaspoon cayenne

WHEN YOU GET THERE: Heat grill to medium-high and let rack get good and hot.

Cut the potatoes lengthwise into wedges about ¾ inch thick at the skins. Mix the melted butter, paprika, salt, and cayenne in a larger zipper-lock bag. Drop in the spuds, and massage to coat all over

Brush and oil grill rack, then grill spuds across the bars until tender inside and nicely grill marked all over, 15 to 20 minutes, turning once or twice. Let cool slightly, then drop the spuds back in the bag and toss to coat with remaining spiced butter. Put onto plates and enjoy.

NEIGHBORLY TIPS You can easily double or triple this recipe.

For extra smoke flavor, replace the cayenne with chipotle powder.

Bruschetta

Only the Italians could make a culinary art form out of toast. In bruschetta (broo-SKEH-ta), sliced bread is grilled over a wood fire, brushed with garlic and olive oil, and topped with chopped tomatoes and basil. To simplify the process for tailgating, I put the olive oil, garlic, tomatoes, and basil into the topping, then just grill the bread. Who wants to brush olive oil onto umpteen bread slices at a tailgate? But, hey, if you want to be authentic, by all means go for it. **MAKES ABOUT 36 SLICES (12 TO 18 SNACK-SIZE SERVINGS)**

¾ cup Italian Tomato Relish (page 38)

1 loaf Italian or French bread (about 1 pound)

BEFORE YOU GO: Make the relish and chill in refrigerator or cooler.

Cut bread crosswise on the diagonal into slices ¼ to ½ inch thick. Seal in large zipper-lock bag and stash in your carry-all bag.

WHEN YOU GET THERE: Remove relish from cooler about 20 minutes before serving. Heat grill to medium and let rack get good and hot. Brush and oil rack, then grill bread until toasted and grill marked, about 2 minutes per side. Watch carefully. These burn up quickly.

Put 1 to 2 teaspoons relish on each slice of grilled bread.

NEIGHBORLY TIPS To save time, you could buy prepared bruschetta topping from the grocery store. Some stores keep it in the cold salad bar, olive bar, or Mediterranean bar.

Anything goes with the topping here. Try Tuscan White Bean Salad (page 42), Tapenade (page 34), sliced smoked mozzarella, dabs of herbed goat cheese, or a combination of cheeses and vegetables.

Black Bean Two-Cheese Quesadillas

Grilled quesadillas are one of my favorite grilled starters. They cook quickly, feed a crowd, and get everybody lubed up while waiting for the big stuff to come off the grill. I usually make the filling ahead of time but you could just as easily do it when you get there. **MAKES 4 QUESADILLAS (ABOUT 8 APPETIZER-SIZE SERVINGS)**

1 can (15 ounces) black beans, rinsed and drained

4 ounces goat cheese or cream cheese

½ cup Simple Salsa (page 39) or your favorite salsa, drained

1 teaspoon chili powder or chipotle powder

2 cups shredded pepper Jack or Cheddar cheese

8 (8-inch) flour tortillas

BEFORE YOU GO: Put beans in medium bowl and mash with fork, leaving some beans whole. Stir in goat or cream cheese, salsa, and chili or chipotle powder. Cover and chill in refrigerator or cooler up to 2 days.

WHEN YOU GET THERE: Remove filling from cooler 20 minutes before grilling. Heat grill to medium and let rack get good and hot.

For each quesadilla, scatter ¼ cup shredded cheese over a tortilla. Spread on one-fourth of filling, then scatter another ¼ cup cheese over filling. Top with a tortilla.

Brush and oil rack, then grill quesadillas until lightly browned and cheese melts, 3 to 5 minutes per side. Cut each quesadilla into 8 wedges.

Pesto Gorgonzola Grilled Pizza

Grilled pizza is a completely different animal from pizzeria pizza. Especially if you grill over a low-burning wood fire. Put on whatever toppings you like best. I like the strong flavors of pesto and Gorgonzola cheese, with a little fresh tomato. Simple. And outrageously delicious. Look for refrigerated pizza dough near the refrigerated biscuits and other tubes of dough in your grocery store. Of course, you could use homemade dough if you have the time to make it. Either way, these pizzas grill up fast, so keep the heat low and take 'em off before they burn. **MAKES 4 SMALL PIZZAS (ABOUT 32 APPETIZER-SIZE SLICES)**

1 cup Basil Pesto (page 35) or commercially prepared pesto

1 large tomato, finely chopped

1½ cups finely crumbled Gorgonzola cheese (or another blue cheese like Stilton or Maytag)

2 cans (10 ounces each) refrigerated pizza dough

BEFORE YOU GO: Make pesto. Chill in refrigerator or cooler.

Chop tomato and put in an airtight container. Chill in refrigerator or cooler.

Put crumbled cheese in an airtight container. Chill in refrigerator or cooler.

Coat four pieces of foil with cooking spray or oil. Unroll each piece of dough and cut each piece in half to make four squares. Put a square on each piece of foil. Press each square into an 8-inch circle on foil. If dough looks irregular, wad it up into a ball and press into a circle. Don't worry about making a big rim around the edge of the crust, but if you like a rim for aesthetics, go ahead. Coat tops of dough with spray or oil and stack up all the rounds of dough. Wrap in plastic and lay flat in top of cooler.

(Note: You could do all this prep at the tailgate, but I like to get a jump on things.)

WHEN YOU GET THERE: Heat grill to medium-low and let rack get good and hot. Brush and oil rack, then invert each circle of dough onto rack and remove foil. Do this in batches unless you have a humongous grill. Cook until just browned on bottom, 1 to 2 minutes. Remove to cutting board with spatula. Invert so grilled side is up. Spread on pesto, then scatter on tomato and cheese. Slide back onto grill with spatula, put down lid, and grill until cheese melts and bottom is browned, about 5 minutes, watching carefully so pizza doesn't burn. Cut each pizza into 8 wedges.

NEIGHBORLY TIP To cut corners, you could use a cooked pizza crust such as Boboli, canned tomatoes, and jarred pesto. It won't be as good, but it'll be good. You'll need about two average-size cooked pizza crusts. Grill the crust top side down, then invert and put on the toppings. Slide back onto the grill to cook the bottom side, as directed in the recipe.

Why Yes, I Do Have Grey Poupon Mustard

The annual summer tailgating event near Santa Fe, New Mexico, would leave most sports fans scratching their heads. People eating sushi, smoked salmon, and arugula salads with goat cheese? Talking about Pavarotti? Drinking *wine*? What kind of tailgating party is this, anyway?

It's opening night at the Santa Fe Opera, of course. Patrons here enjoy an annual tradition of dining out near the opera house before opening-night performances. They eat gourmet food from their china, crystal, and good silverware. The men often wear tuxes, and many women wear their best gowns—though some people wear denim couture that's more befitting a football tailgating party.

Roughly 2,100 attended the opera party in 2004, after which they adjourned to root for . . . er, cheer on . . . well actually just *watch* Verdi's *Simon Boccanegra*.

This year's classy get-together brought out many emotions from the well-heeled attendees. As one told a local newspaper reporter, "Opera night is a magical night." Another made the scene for different reasons: "I wanted to come because it sounded so ridiculous."

Chicken Pesto Panini

Panini is Italian for "small bread," meaning a little sandwich. Here, the sandwich gets a bit bigger with grilled chicken, sliced ham, roasted peppers, pesto, and provolone. Yum! The whole thing is grilled under a brick or other heavy weight. It's a cool sight to see and the sandwich picks up awesome flavor from the grill.

MAKES 4 SANDWICHES

2 large boneless, skinless chicken breasts, about 1 pound total

6 tablespoons Basil Pesto (page 35) or jarred pesto

8 slices sourdough bread

8 slices provolone cheese, preferably smoked

8 thin slices deli ham

1 jar (4 ounces) roasted red peppers, drained

1 tablespoon olive oil

BEFORE YOU GO: The morning of the tailgate, put a chicken breast between sheets of plastic wrap and pound with a heavy skillet to an even ¼-inch thickness. Cut pounded chicken in half. Repeat with other chicken breast. Spread 2 tablespoons pesto over all four pounded chicken pieces, then stack them up. Wrap in plastic and chill in refrigerator or cooler.

WHEN YOU GET THERE: Heat grill to medium and let rack get good and hot.

Spread remaining ¼ cup pesto over one side of sliced bread. Put a slice of provolone over each piece of bread. Layer ham and roasted peppers over four of the bread pieces (the sandwich bottoms).

Brush and oil grill rack, then grill chicken until nicely grill marked and no longer pink in center, 3 to 5 minutes per side, turning when chicken turns white around edges. Put chicken over roasted peppers on sandwich bottoms. Top with other slice of bread, press sandwiches down gently, and brush outsides with oil or coat with spray.

Grill sandwiches with a heavy weight on top, such as a cast-iron pan or foil-wrapped brick, until nicely grill-marked and cheese melts, 3 to 5 minutes per side.

Cut in half on the diagonal and serve.

NEIGHBORLY TIPS If you can't find authentic sourdough bread, Pepperidge Farm makes sliced sourdough bread in a bag. Look for it in the bread aisle. Or use a sturdy, country-style white or Italian bread.

Whole dill pickles make a great accompaniment here. And potato chips. Just like in the sandwich shops!

NBC Ruins an Entire Game

Fans who attended the Jets-Raiders game in Oakland on Nov. 17, 1968, got to see something that the folks viewing at home missed: a little thing called the end of the game!

The match went back and forth each quarter, and with 1:05 minutes remaining, New York held a close lead. The game was running long, so a honcho at NBC then made a move that still holds a place in the Annals of Dumb Decisions: the network cut to a commercial and cued up the movie *Heidi*.

As stunned fans at home watched the fictional adventures of the little Swiss girl, the Raiders rallied ahead to a 43–32 victory.

To be fair, one reviewer of the *Heidi* program noted that "some of the scenes between Heidi and her grandfather and uncle are quite touching." This was little comfort to the angry fans who swamped the NBC switchboard. Their ire forced the network to publicly apologize.

Grilled Calzones

If you keep the heat low, a covered kettle grill can double as an oven. These calzones are made just like the ones you get from pizza shop ovens, but on the grill. I use refrigerated pizza dough for convenience; if you have a favorite dough, go ahead and use that. I also use provolone cheese in place of the more common mozzarella. Plain ol' sliced provolone and deli ham work fine here. **MAKES 4 MEDIUM CAL-ZONES (ENOUGH TO FEED 8 PEOPLE OR 4 REALLY HUNGRY FANS)**

½ pound smoked ham, finely chopped

½ pound provolone cheese, finely chopped

2 cups ricotta cheese

½ cup grated Parmesan cheese

1 teaspoon Italian seasoning

2 cans (10 ounces each) refrigerated pizza dough

2 cups Basic Tomato-Basil Sauce (page 117) or your favorite
tomato sauce, optional

BEFORE YOU GO: Mix together ham, provolone, ricotta, Parmesan, and Italian seasoning in large bowl. Spoon into large zipper-lock bag and chill in refrigerator or cooler.

Coat four pieces of foil with cooking spray or oil. Unroll each piece of dough and cut each piece in half to make four squares. Put a square on each piece of foil. Press each square into a 9-inch circle of even thickness on foil. If dough looks irregular, wad it up into a ball and press into a circle. Coat tops of dough with spray or oil. Stack up, then wrap in plastic and lay flat in top of cooler.

(Note: You could do all this prep at the tailgate, but I like to do it ahead.)

WHEN YOU GET THERE: Remove filling from cooler 20 minutes before grilling. Put tomato sauce, if using, in small saucepan over low heat to keep warm.

Heat grill to medium-low (more on the low side) and let rack get good and hot.

Mound one-fourth of filling onto one side of each round of dough. Pull dough over filling and seal edges with your fingers. Coat tops with cooking spray or oil.

Brush and oil grill rack. Working in batches if you have a small grill, carefully invert each calzone onto grill rack and remove foil. Cover and grill until nicely browned, 2 to 4 minutes per side, flipping once with a long spatula. Watch, these brown quickly. Remove to a cutting board and let rest 5 minutes. Serve whole or cut in half on a diagonal with tomato sauce on side for dipping.

A Broken Snout

Packers and Bears fans have more in common than their brutal northern winters: they also share a fierce rivalry that some say dates back to 1921. The Bears—back then known by the much less fierce name of "the Staleys"—tromped the first-season Packers 20–0. During the game, a Staleys guard gave a Packers tackle a cheap shot in the face, breaking his nose. The shot has reverberated down through the generations, and fans of the two teams carry a well-known disdain for each other to this day.

Brats in Beer

Some tailgaters grill their brats and serve 'em up right away in buns. This method gives you a crisp skin and lets you choose your favorite toppings, as you would with a hot dog. I prefer to grill the brats, then let them stew in a mixture of beer, bell pepper, onion, and sauerkraut. The beer softens the grilled skin a bit, but the brats stay moist and get a more complex flavor from the stew. More important, you can let the brats sit in the pan on the grill for hours in case you happen to get a little too stewed yourself to keep watch over them. If you're at Soldier Field for a Chicago Bears home game or at Lambeau Field for a Packers game, you'll fit right in with these brats on the grill. **MAKES 10 BRATS**

2½ pounds of your favorite fresh bratwurst (about 10 links)

2 cups sauerkraut, drained

1 bottle or can (12 ounces) beer

1 green bell pepper, cut into short strips

1 onion, thinly sliced

4 tablespoons (½ stick) butter or vegetable oil, optional

10 crusty sausage or steak rolls

½ cup coarse German mustard

WHEN YOU GET THERE: Heat grill to medium and let rack get good and hot, about 10 minutes. Brush and oil rack, then grill brats until nicely browned all over, turning now and then, 15 to 20 minutes total. Put brats in a large disposable aluminum pan directly on grill. Mix in kraut, beer, bell pepper, onion, and butter or oil, if using. Stew in pan (on the grill), mixing occasionally, for at least 30 minutes or up to 3 hours (for a charcoal grill, add fresh coals every hour or so). Serve on rolls with a steaming slew of kraut, peppers, onions, and a thick band of mustard.

NEIGHBORLY TIPS Brat (pronounced BRAHT) is short for bratwurst, a type of German sausage that's usually made from coarsely ground pork (and sometimes veal) that's seasoned with salt, pepper, and a mix of "sweet" spices like nutmeg. If you have a German-American butcher in your area, go there for fresh brats. Or pick up a brand-name bratwurst such as Johnsonville from the sausage section of your grocery store. If you're feeling health conscious, look for reduced-fat turkey bratwurst.

I like crusty, untoasted rolls for bratwurst. The outside of the roll gives you good crunch and the soft interior soaks up all the stewy juices from the brats. But if you're using generic pillowy hot dog buns, toast them first (on the grill) to crisp them up. That will help keep the buns from turning to mush under the brats and stew juices.

If you like your brats with a crisp skin but still want the stewed flavor, reverse the cooking process in this recipe. Stew the brats in the pan with the other ingredients first; then when you're ready, toss them on the grill until the skins are browned all over and the brats are cooked through.

Try this recipe with a mix of sausages like knackwurst, kielbasa, and mild or hot Italian sausage.

Big Brats

Johnsonville, Wisconsin, may be home to the nation's best-known bratwurst. But the biggest brat is over in neighboring Campbellsport. On July 3, 2004, Loehr's Meat Service of Campbellsport, Wisconsin, made the world's biggest brat, a single sausage link nearly 40 feet in length. The champion sausage was placed in a 40-foot bun and cut into 120 portions selling for $10 each in honor of the Campbellsport Fire Department's 100th anniversary. A local supermarket supplied the condiments.

Rum-Cardamom Pork Chops

When I was testing this recipe, my biker pal Mark Taylor had this to say: "These chops are bangin'!" It's always good when a recipe hits home with the testers. These thick chops are rubbed with a Caribbean-inspired mix of cardamom, coriander, paprika, and cinnamon. They're quick to put together before you leave for the game, then when you get there, just fire up the grill, brush the chops with sauce, and enjoy. Break out the piña coladas! **MAKES 4 SERVINGS**

SPICE RUB

1 tablespoon dark brown sugar

1 tablespoon ground cardamom

2 teaspoons ground coriander

2 teaspoons salt

1 teaspoon paprika

½ teaspoon cinnamon

½ teaspoon ground black pepper

CHOPS

2 tablespoons dark rum

1 tablespoon vegetable oil

2 garlic cloves, minced

4 bone-in pork loin chops (each about 1 inch thick and 10 to 12 ounces)

1½ cups Basic Barbecue Sauce (page 114) or your favorite barbecue sauce

BEFORE YOU GO: Make the barbecue sauce (or plan to bring your own). The morning of the tailgate, mix spice rub ingredients in small bowl. Set aside 1 tablespoon of rub and mix it with rum, oil, and garlic in a small zipper-lock bag. Seal and chill in refrigerator or cooler. Scatter remaining spice mix all over chops and pat into meat. Put rubbed chops in large freezer-weight zipper-lock bag, seal, and chill in refrigerator or cooler.

WHEN YOU GET THERE: Pull chops from cooler 20 minutes before grilling. Heat grill to medium-high and let rack get good and hot. Brush and oil rack, then grill chops until nicely browned on both sides, 6 to 8 minutes per side, basting each side with reserved rum mixture. During last 5 minutes of grilling, brush both sides of chops with barbecue sauce. When done, chops should be firm but slightly yielding when poked, about 155°F on an instant-read thermometer inserted through the side of a chop.

Serve with remaining barbecue sauce.

NEIGHBORLY TIP If you're out of barbecue sauce, don't worry. The chops taste damn good without it. But I like that final splash of moisture and flavor, especially if you happen to get some subpar chops.

Broncomaniacs

You think *you* have a hard time getting to the stadium on game day? Meet the Cordells. They'll make you realize your commute isn't so bad.

Craig and Karen Cordell are Denver Broncos season ticket holders, and they've faithfully attended the games in Colorado for the past ten years. Unfortunately, they live in tiny Inkom, Idaho, which is more than six hundred miles away. It's not even a neighboring state!

The couple has won the Denver Broncos' Tailgater of the Year award, largely on the basis of one telling photograph. The picture shows the Cordells on Interstate 80 in the middle of a Wyoming blizzard that created a fourteen-hour trip, one-way. "People were really impressed with that. Even fans who live in Denver say, 'We don't want to drive across town to the game when roads are bad,' " Craig says. At that game, ten thousand people were no-shows.

The couple, married for fourteen years, makes the trip in a pickup outfitted with a camper, which has a toilet, heavy-duty heater, stove, refrigerator, and bed. So they're not too worried about getting stranded on the road, which has happened.

Smoky Rubbed Ribs

I brought these to an early-season tailgate and everybody went nuts over them. The key is using lots of wood smoke and slow-grilling the ribs so they don't dry out or burn. This takes about 1½ hours. Start 'em early if you plan to make it to the game. There's a bit of prep involved the night before, and it really helps to use a rib rack, a cheap metal contraption available at most hardware stores. Your efforts will be rewarded with awesome-tasting ribs and major kudos from your tailgate buddies. These are pretty mild (not spicy). For spicy ribs, see the next recipe. **MAKES 4 BIG SERVINGS OR 8 MEDIUM SERVINGS**

¼ cup celery salt

¼ cup paprika

¼ cup packed dark brown sugar

2 tablespoons dry mustard

1 teaspoon garlic powder

1 teaspoon onion powder

½ teaspoon cayenne

½ teaspoon ground black pepper

4 racks baby-back pork ribs, membrane removed

2 cups Basic Barbecue Sauce (page 114) or your favorite barbecue sauce

2 cups wood chips (hickory, oak, or applewood)

BEFORE YOU GO: The night before, mix together everything but ribs, barbecue sauce, and wood chips in medium bowl. Rinse ribs, then pat dry with paper towels. Scatter spice rub over ribs, patting it in with your fingers. Put in big, strong plastic bags (2-gallon freezer-weight zipper-lock bags will hold two racks each). Seal and chill overnight in refrigerator or cooler.

Make barbecue sauce (or plan to bring your own). Transfer to airtight container and chill in refrigerator or cooler.

The morning of the tailgate, put wood chips and enough cold water to cover in freezer-weight zipper-lock bag. Seal and chill in cooler for 1 hour. Or if your cooler's full, soak the chips at the game in a bag or bucket.

WHEN YOU GET THERE: If it's cold out, put barbecue sauce in small pot and heat on low to keep warm (cold sauce would slow the cooking of the meat). Otherwise, pull sauce and ribs from cooler about 20 minutes before grilling. Heat grill to medium-low (300° to 325°F). If using charcoal, spread hot coals to opposite sides, leaving a large unheated space in middle. Brush and oil grill rack. Drain about 1 cup wood chips and scatter ½ cup over coals on each side. If using gas, drain all of wood chips and put in smoker box or in foil directly over one of the heated burners (see page 28). Heat gas grill to high until you see lots of smoke, then turn heat to medium-low. Turn off middle burner(s), or if you only have two burners, turn off the burner that doesn't have the wood chips over it.

Put ribs in a metal rib rack over unheated part of grill. If you don't have a metal rib rack, put ribs directly over unheated part of grill in batches (which will extend the total cooking time). Cover and cook until ribs are well browned, tender, and shrunken back from ends of bones, 1½ to 2 hours. During last 30 minutes, use basting brush to dab ribs all over once or twice with barbecue sauce. If using charcoal, add fresh coals and remaining wood chips after an hour or so.

Put ribs on cutting board and let rest 5 minutes. Cut into individual servings and serve with leftover barbecue sauce.

NEIGHBORLY TIPS Most grocery-store baby-backs will come with the membrane removed from the meaty side of the ribs. If your ribs still have skin attached to the meaty side, ask your butcher to remove it. Or do it yourself: Use a flat blunt object (like a clean screwdriver) to lift up the skin from one corner of the ribs and wiggle it loose. Grip the skin with a kitchen towel and pull the whole sheet of membrane off the meat.

If you have a smoker instead of a charcoal grill, smoke the ribs at 225°F for about 3 hours.

Chipotle-Bourbon Ribs

These are serious ribs for those who like to put a little effort into great barbecue. Ribs can be dry, so I keep them moist by using the more succulent baby-backs instead of spareribs. These babies are marinated in apple cider and bourbon, rubbed with a hot chipotle chile pepper spice mix, doused with cider and bourbon during cooking, and slathered with sweet, smoky chipotle-bourbon barbecue sauce at the end of cooking. If you happen to be at Arrowhead Stadium for a Kansas City Chiefs game, you'll mesh well with the resident barbecuers there. Chiefs fans usually cook up sweet and sticky ribs like these, rather than the dry-rubbed ribs you find in Memphis. The difference here is a little Texas-style kick and Kentucky-style whiskey. **MAKES 8 MEDIUM SERVINGS OR 4 BIG SERVINGS**

1 quart apple cider

1 cup bourbon

4 racks baby-back pork ribs, membrane removed

3 cups Rich, Sweet, and Smoky Chipotle-Bourbon Barbecue Sauce (page 115)

¼ cup salt

¼ cup packed dark brown sugar

¼ cup paprika

2 tablespoons chipotle powder

2 tablespoons dry mustard

1 teaspoon ground cumin

2 cups wood chips (applewood, hickory, or oak)

BEFORE YOU GO: The night before, mix together cider and bourbon in large glass measure or bowl. Pour 1 cup of mixture into small, clean spray bottle and refrigerate. Rinse ribs, then pat dry with paper towels. Put ribs in big, strong plastic bags (2-gallon freezer-weight zipper-lock bags will hold two racks each). Pour remaining cider-bourbon mixture into bags. Seal and chill overnight in refrigerator or cooler.

Make barbecue sauce (or plan to bring your own). Transfer to airtight container and chill in refrigerator or cooler.

The morning of the tailgate, mix salt, brown sugar, paprika, chipotle powder, dry mustard, and cumin in medium bowl. Remove ribs from bag and pat dry with paper towels. Discard marinade and bags. Scatter spice rub over ribs, patting it in with your fingers. Slide ribs into fresh bags, seal, and chill in cooler for at least 1 hour.

Put wood chips and enough cold water to cover in freezer-weight zipper-lock bag. Seal and chill in cooler for 1 hour. Or if your cooler's full, soak the chips at the game in a bag or bucket.

WHEN YOU GET THERE: If it's cold out, put barbecue sauce in small pot and heat on low to keep warm (cold sauce would slow the cooking of the meat). Otherwise, don't bother. Pull sauce, ribs, and spray bottle from cooler about 20 minutes before grilling. Heat grill to medium-low (300° to 325°F). If using charcoal, spread hot coals to opposite sides, leaving a large unheated space in middle. Brush and oil grill rack. Drain about 1 cup wood chips and scatter ½ cup over coals on each side. If using gas, drain all of wood chips and put in smoker box or in foil directly over one of the heated burners (see page 28). Heat gas grill to high until you see lots of smoke, then turn heat to medium-low. Turn off middle burner(s), or if you only have two burners, turn off the burner that doesn't have the pouch over it.

Put ribs in a metal rib rack over unheated part of grill. If you don't have a metal rib rack, put ribs directly over unheated part of grill in batches (which will extend the total cooking time). Cover and cook until ribs are well browned, tender, and shrunken back from ends of bones, 1½ to 2 hours. Spray ribs with reserved cider-bourbon mixture every 20 minutes or so to keep meat moist. During last 30 minutes, brush ribs all over once or twice with barbecue sauce. If using charcoal, add fresh coals and remaining wood chips after an hour or so.

Put ribs on cutting board and let rest 5 minutes. Cut into individual servings and serve with leftover barbecue sauce.

NEIGHBORLY TIPS If you have a smoker instead of a charcoal grill, smoke the ribs at 225°F for about 3 hours.

Ground chipotle chiles (smoke-dried red jalapeño peppers) are available in the spice aisle of most grocery stores. Look among the "gourmet" spices kept in glass bottles.

This chipotle spice rub is hot. If you wear contact lenses, put on gloves before rubbing the spices into the meat. Or use only one hand to rub in the spices and never touch your eyes or contacts with that hand.

You'll need a metal rib rack to fit all four baby-backs on a typical kettle grill at once. Most hardware stores and home centers sell metal rib racks for about ten bucks. If you're only serving two to four people, cut the recipe in half and put the two baby-backs right on the grill rack. You'll also need a small spray bottle for spritzing the ribs with the cider-bourbon mixture. Use a clean one from home or pick up one at a hardware store.

What's a Scoville Unit?

Thanks to pharmacist Wilbur Scoville, we now have a scale to scientifically measure the pungency of a hot pepper. Sweet Italian bell peppers rate a wimpy 0 "Scoville units" on the scale. The chipotle and jalapeño chiles can bring tears to your eyes with 2,500 or up to 10,000 Scoville units. And a Scotch bonnet or habanero can make you feel the burn for days with a 300,000-Scoville unit scorch.

Pure capsaicin, the stuff that gives a chile pepper its heat, registers at a surface-of-the-sun 16 million Scoville units. Here are ratings for some of the hottest hot sauces available, plus a few mild ones for reference.

Hot Sauce	Scoville Units
Tabasco	2,500
El Yucateco Chile Habanero (Green)	8,000
Endorphin Rush Beyond	33,000
Dave's Insanity	51,000
Dave's Ultimate Insanity	90,000
Dead Heat Limited Edition	100,000
Da Bomb—The Final Answer	1,500,000
Blair's 6am	12,000,000+

Carolina Pulled Pork

The Carolinas aren't just home to great college and pro football teams. They own one of the best hot sandwiches ever made in America: pulled pork. The cut of meat is usually pork butt, otherwise known as a bone-in shoulder roast. And in the Carolinas, the sauce is typically heavy on the vinegar and spice. There are loads of variations on spice rubs and sauces that go with "proper" pulled pork. Most rubs include a mix of ground mild and hot chile peppers with a little sugar, salt, and other seasonings. The sauces tend to be high in vinegar with solid doses of salt, chile peppers, and a touch of sweetness to balance out the flavors. Here's my take on this classic American sandwich. I like some ketchup in the sauce, western Carolina style. Keep in mind that slow-grilling a pork butt takes about 5 hours. But you'll get some damn good pull when it's done! **MAKES ABOUT 12 SANDWICHES**

SAUCE

2 cups cider vinegar

¾ cup ketchup

½ cup water

2 tablespoons sugar

1 tablespoon mild hot pepper sauce (such as Frank's)

2 teaspoons salt

1 teaspoon crushed red pepper flakes

½ teaspoon ground black pepper

RUB AND PORK

2 tablespoons sweet paprika

1 tablespoon light brown sugar

2 teaspoons salt

1 teaspoon ground black pepper

1 teaspoon cayenne

1 teaspoon onion powder

1 teaspoon dry mustard

(continued)

1 bone-in pork shoulder roast (a.k.a. Boston butt) (6 to 7 pounds)

1 pound coleslaw mix (shredded green cabbage and carrots), optional

12 hamburger buns

5 cups wood chips (hickory is best)

BEFORE YOU GO: The night before, mix sauce ingredients in medium glass or ceramic bowl. Microwave 1 minute to warm up sauce and dissolve salt and sugar. Stir, then set aside ½ cup of the sauce to mix with the coleslaw, if using. Pour both portions into zipper-lock bags. Seal and chill in refrigerator or cooler.

Mix rub ingredients in 2-gallon freezer-weight zipper-lock bag. Scatter rub over pork, patting it in with your fingers. If you have any rub left over, mix it into the sauce. Put spiced pork into 2-gallon bag that contained the spice rub. Seal and chill in refrigerator or cooler overnight.

The morning of the tailgate, put wood chips and enough cold water to cover in freezer-weight zipper-lock bag. Seal and chill in cooler for 1 hour. Or if your cooler's full, soak the chips at the game in a bag or bucket.

WHEN YOU GET THERE: Remove pork from cooler about 20 minutes before grilling. Heat grill to medium-low (300° to 325°F). If using charcoal, spread hot coals to opposite sides, and drop a large disposable aluminum drip pan in empty space in middle. Brush and oil grill rack. Drain about 1 cup wood chips and scatter ½ cup over coals on each side. If using gas, drain all of wood chips and put in smoker box or in foil directly over one of the heated burners (see page 28). Heat gas grill to high until you see lots of smoke, then turn heat to medium-low. Turn off middle burner(s), or if you only have two burners, turn off the burner that doesn't have the woodships over it.

Put seasoned pork butt, fatty side up, over unheated part of grill (over drip pan). Cover and cook until pork is dark all over and fall-apart tender (about 190°F on an instant-read thermometer), 4 to 5 hours total. If using charcoal, add fresh coals and remaining wood chips when the old ones die out, about once an hour.

While pork cooks, pour reserved ½ cup sauce into large bowl. Mix in coleslaw mix, if using, until thoroughly coated.

Rest meat off heat to let juices redistribute, about 20 minutes. Using a fork or your fingers, pull pork into shreds, breaking up crispy bits and discarding bones or excess fat. Put shredded pork in large disposable aluminum pan (not the drip pan already used) with about 2 cups of sauce. Put pan back on center of grill or cover with foil to keep warm. Pile a big mound of pork and some coleslaw, if using, on each bun. Drizzle on more sauce to taste.

NEIGHBORLY TIPS If your idea of pork barbecue includes a sweeter, smokier barbecue sauce, mix your favorite barbecue sauce into half of the sauce called for here. Or just follow the recipe, then pour some barbecue sauce onto your sandwich.

The slaw is optional but traditional on Carolina pulled pork sandwiches. If you like a creamier, less vinegary slaw, try the Creamy Slaw on page 41.

Coleslaw mix is available in the bagged salad section of most grocery stores.

If you have a smoker instead of a charcoal grill, smoke the pork at 225°F for about 8 hours.

Buffalo Burgers

Ground buffalo (bison) is very lean—about 75 percent leaner than ground beef. With so little fat, the meat cooks very quickly. To keep the meat's juices from vaporizing, always grill buffalo over medium-low heat. I like to mix in a few seasonings for extra flavor. You can use whatever mix of spices you like, but try to keep the three basic elements: salt, pepper, and sugar. When these burgers are done the way you like them, pile on the condiments. **MAKES 8 BURGERS**

> 2 pounds ground buffalo
>
> 4 teaspoons salt
>
> 4 teaspoons paprika
>
> 2 teaspoons dark brown sugar
>
> 2 teaspoons ground black pepper

BEFORE YOU GO: Using your hands, gently mix all ingredients in medium bowl. Shape into 8 patties, each about ½ inch thick. Put burgers between layers of wax paper and cover with wax paper. Store in airtight, crushproof container and chill in refrigerator or cooler up to 2 days.

WHEN YOU GET THERE: Remove burgers from cooler 20 minutes before grilling. Heat grill to medium-low and let rack get good and hot. Brush and oil rack, then grill burgers until slightly pink in center for medium-rare, 5 to 6 minutes per side (about 145°F on an instant-read thermometer), or until no longer pink in center for medium (about 160°F), 7 to 8 minutes per side.

NEIGHBORLY TIPS More farmers' markets and butchers are selling buffalo meat. If you can't find any in your area, check the sources beginning on page 184. Or look on the Internet for a source near you.

Serve these burgers with your favorite rolls, toasted on the grill. And, of course, piled high with condiments: ketchup, mayo, lettuce, tomato, onion, etc. If you've got other veggies, like mushrooms or peppers, in the cooler, toss them on the grill with the burgers, then slice 'em to use as a topping.

Cook your opponent! Put these buffalo burgers on the grill when your NFL team is up against the Buffalo Bills or when your college team has a home game with the University of Colorado (their mascot is a buffalo).

NASCAR Tailgating

If you think football tailgating is the biggest party for sports fans, check out a NASCAR race sometime. The first thing you'll notice is the sheer number of people.

While the biggest football stadium lots fill up with 50,000 or even 100,000 tailgaters, it's typical for NASCAR tailgates to host 150,000 to 200,000 people at each event. That's because football games are only between two teams, but at a NASCAR event, more than forty drivers will be racing, and each one will draw a crowd of fans. "It would be as if all the teams in the NFL played at once," says Jo Anne Hlavac, a longtime NASCAR fan from Charleston, South Carolina, who runs the www.laidbackracing.com Web site with her husband, Jimmy.

"And nothing against tailgaters at football games," she adds, "but they usually get there the day of the football game. We start tailgating a *week* ahead of time. People literally plan their whole vacations around going to a race."

The Hlavacs' tailgating group fires up a deep-fat fryer, a gas grill, and a smoker for the feast. "People tell me they eat better with us than when they eat at home," she says. Besides the food, typical NASCAR fan festivities include drinking, of course, and a game called washers, which is similar to a bean-bag toss but uses round metal washers instead.

The answer to rising ticket prices, Hlavac says, is to stretch out the adventure with tailgating. Ticket prices seem much more reasonable when you get several days of enjoyment out of the event. "That's one reason why we show up so early," she says, "so we can justify the money we're spending."

Buffalo Fajitas

If you want to grill up a decent lunch before a noon game, try this recipe. You marinate a steak the night before, then grill it for 15 minutes and serve it up with your favorite fajita fixin's. Beef skirt steak is traditional for fajitas. Here, I switch things up and use buffalo, which is perfect for games against the Buffalo Bills. When you can't beat 'em, eat 'em! The marinade here is classic Tex-Mex: beer, lime, garlic, chili powder, and cumin. The key thing to remember is that buffalo meat is very lean and cooks quickly. Keep the grill at medium-low. If you can't get buffalo steaks, use beef skirt steak or flank steak instead. Marinate as directed and grill over medium heat instead of medium-low for an extra 5 to 10 minutes. **MAKES 8 FAJITAS**

1 cup beer

½ cup vegetable oil

Juice of 2 limes

3 tablespoons Worcestershire sauce

4 garlic cloves, minced

2 tablespoons chili powder

1 teaspoon ground cumin

2 teaspoons Tabasco, or more to taste

2 to 2½ pounds buffalo skirt or flank steak

1 teaspoon salt

8 flour tortillas

2 cups Simple Salsa (page 39) or your favorite salsa

¾ cup sour cream, optional

BEFORE YOU GO: The night before, put beer, oil, lime juice, Worcestershire, garlic, chili powder, cumin, and Tabasco in a large freezer-weight zipper-lock bag. Drop in steak, seal, and chill in refrigerator or cooler overnight. When using skirt steak, open up the entire steak to expose all surfaces to the marinade.

WHEN YOU GET THERE: Remove steak from cooler 20 minutes before grilling. Heat grill to medium-low and let rack get good and hot. Brush and oil rack, then unfold steak onto rack and grill, covered, for 4 to 6 minutes per side for medium-rare (140° to 145°F on an instant-read thermometer), or 8 to 10 minutes per side for medium (160° to 165°F on an instant-read thermometer). Sprinkle each side with ½ teaspoon salt during grilling.

Rest steak off heat for 10 minutes to let juices redistribute.

Wrap tortillas in foil and grill until heated through, 3 to 4 minutes per side.

Slice steak across grain into ⅛-inch-thick slices. Roll up in warm tortillas with salsa and sour cream, if using.

NEIGHBORLY TIPS Skirt steak is a long, narrow, flat strip of meat cut from the diaphragm of the animal. When grilling, open the skirt all the way so it lies flat on the grill.

While you're at the grill, toss on some onions and peppers to go with the fajitas (2 to 3 of each should do it). Peel the onions, then cut them in half. Cut the peppers into quarters, then remove the seeds and cores. Grill the onions and peppers over medium heat until blackened in spots and still a little crunchy, about 5 minutes. If you have any vegetable oil on hand, brush the veggies with a little oil to keep 'em moist. Slice the grilled veggies into strips and serve with the fajitas.

For extra smoke flavor, soak about 1 cup wood chips (like hickory or mesquite) for 1 hour, then toss on the hot coals.

Beer and Coffee Steaks

Want to get fired up for the game? Have some coffee with your grilled steak. Better yet, on your grilled steak. Wait, let's go one better and marinate the steaks in beer first! Coffee-rubbed steaks have been getting popular all over the United States. This is my spicy, Texas-style version with dark beer and dark coffee. **MAKES 4 BIG STEAKS**

12 ounces dark beer, such as Negra Modelo

¼ cup Worcestershire sauce

1 tablespoon Tabasco

4 boneless strip steaks (1½ to 2 pounds), trimmed of fat

3 tablespoons finely ground espresso or dark roast coffee

1 tablespoon pure chile powder (such as ancho)

1 teaspoon ground cumin

1 teaspoon sugar

½ teaspoon cayenne, or more to taste

1 teaspoon salt

½ teaspoon ground black pepper

BEFORE YOU GO: The night before, mix beer, Worcestershire, and Tabasco in large freezer-weight zipper-lock bag. Put steaks in bag, seal, and chill in refrigerator or cooler overnight.

The next morning, mix remaining ingredients in small bowl. Remove steaks from marinade and discard marinade. Pat steaks dry with paper towels, then scatter spice mix over steaks, patting it in with your fingers. Slip into clean zipper-lock bags, seal, and chill in cooler.

WHEN YOU GET THERE: Remove steaks from cooler about 20 minutes before grilling. Heat grill to high and let rack get good and hot. Brush and oil rack, then grill steaks until darkly crusted and done the way you like, about 3 minutes per side for medium-rare (about 145°F on an instant-read thermometer), or 4 to 5 minutes per side for medium (about 160°F on an instant-read thermometer). Let meat rest off heat 5 minutes to redistribute juices.

NEIGHBORLY TIPS Most grocery stores carry espresso or dark roast coffee beans. Grind them in the store's grinder or at home for even better freshness. You could also get the beans ground at your favorite coffee shop.

Look for pure ancho chile powder in the spice aisle of your grocery store. It's usually kept with the fancy spices in the glass bottles. If you can't find it, use commercial chili powder and omit the cumin (commercial chili powder usually contains cumin).

A small chunk of butter finishes this steak off nicely. Toss it on just before eating and let it melt all over the steak. Or serve with your favorite steak sauce.

Moderate Drinking May Sharpen Your Wits

Alcohol isn't generally thought of as a brain-booster. Anyone who's said something stooopid or made a bad wager after a few beers can vouch for that. But according to research from the land whose "football" is our soccer, having a few drinks each week might actually help to sharpen your wits.

In a study reported in 2004, researchers from the University College of London gave a series of mental function tests to more than 6,000 middle-aged people. Those who had at least one drink in the past week—including beer—were "significantly less likely to have poor cognitive function." Surprisingly, this included those who drank 30 drinks per week!

Other research has shown that one to two drinks per day may help protect against coronary heart disease and the most common form of stroke. However, scientists never want their studies to be used to encourage overconsumption. It's well documented that *too much* alcohol can flog your liver, cause regrettable behavior, and make you crash your car, among other things.

Still, when you're going to have to use your brain   say, while picking players for your fantasy football team—having a beer in your hand may be helpful.

Tequila Tri-Tip

Mike Hammett is a Raiders fan from Seattle who loves his tri-tip, a triangular cut of beef from the tip of the sirloin. Mike inspired me to make this tequila-marinated version with a cumin-oregano rub in honor of the Raider Nation. Tri-tip is something of a regional cut, widely available on the West Coast, less so in the east. You'll find it all over the Coliseum parking lot at Oakland Raiders home games. If you can't find it in your grocery store, ask your butcher to cut the tri-tips for you. If that fails, ask for two 2-pound cuts of bottom sirloin, each 2½ to 3 inches thick—a reasonable approximation of the tri-tip. Some grocery stores sell these cuts as "sirloin roast." The key is that the cut comes from the bottom sirloin rather than the top. The bottom sirloin is a tougher—but more flavorful—cut of meat. **MAKES 12 SERVINGS**

Juice of 2 limes

½ cup tequila

½ cup chopped fresh cilantro

¼ cup olive oil

¼ cup soy sauce

6 garlic cloves, finely chopped

1 tablespoon dried oregano

2 teaspoons ground cumin

1 teaspoon ground black pepper

2 beef loin tri-tip roasts (each 2 to 2½ pounds)

1 teaspoon salt

1 teaspoon paprika

4 cups Simple Salsa (page 39) or your favorite salsa

2 cups wood chips (oak or hickory)

BEFORE YOU GO: The night before, put a large freezer-weight zipper-lock bag in a colander or bowl to hold it up. Add lime juice, tequila, cilantro, oil, soy sauce, garlic, 1 teaspoon of the oregano, ½ teaspoon of the cumin, and ½ teaspoon of the pepper. Shake to mix. Fill a kitchen syringe with some marinade, then inject into roasts in several places. If you don't have a kitchen syringe, pierce roasts all over with a small sharp knife. Drop roasts into bag of remaining marinade, seal, and refrigerate overnight.

The next morning, transfer roasts to a cutting board and discard marinade. Pat roasts dry with paper towels. Mix together remaining 2 teaspoons oregano, 1½ teaspoons cumin, ½ teaspoon pepper, the salt, and paprika. Scatter over roasts, rubbing it in with your fingers. Put roasts into a fresh bag, seal, and chill in cooler.

Put wood chips and enough cold water to cover in freezer-weight zipper-lock bag. Seal and chill in cooler for 1 hour. Or if your cooler's full, soak the chips at the game in a bag or bucket.

WHEN YOU GET THERE: Remove tri-tip from cooler about 20 minutes before grilling. Heat grill to medium-high. If using charcoal, push coals into one high side and one low side of coals for medium-high and medium-low heat zones. Drain all of wood chips and scatter over coals on each side. If using gas, drain all of wood chips and put in smoker box or in foil directly over one of the heated burners (see page 28). Heat gas grill to high until you see lots of smoke, then turn heat to medium-low. Turn off middle burner(s), or if you only have two burners, turn off the burner that doesn't have the wood chips over it. Serve with the salsa.

Brush and oil grill rack, then let it get good and hot. Grill roasts, covered, over medium-high heat until medium-rare, 10 to 12 minutes per side, 30 to 40 minutes total. The meat should register about 140°F on an instant-read thermometer. If roasts start to burn before cooking through, move them to medium-low heat zone to finish cooking.

Rest meat off heat to let juices redistribute, about 10 minutes. Slice across the grain.

NEIGHBORLY TIPS Serve with Barbecue Beans (page 116).

If you can't find oak wood chips, but have a big ol' oak tree nearby, break up some thin, dry branches and toss them right on the coals.

Cold leftovers make great roast beef sandwiches. Slice the meat thinly and serve on crusty rolls with horseradish or your favorite fixings.

Look for kitchen syringes, also called marinade injectors, at cookware stores or at The Barbecue Store, listed in the sources on page 182.

Beer-Mopped Brisket with Texas Barbecue Sauce

Brisket is a tough, fatty cut of meat from the lower breast of the steer. Long cooking over low heat transforms this chewy slab of beef into a moist and tender slice of heaven. On the grill, that means at least 5 hours of cooking. If you're planning to spend the day in the parking lot, this is the perfect recipe. It needs only minor tending and turns out great barbecue that will easily feed you and ten of your friends. The flavorings here are pure Texas: hot and spicy. **MAKES 10 TO 12 SERVINGS**

SPICE RUB

¼ cup paprika
¼ cup light brown sugar
2 tablespoons salt
2 tablespoons chili powder
2 teaspoons garlic powder
1 teaspoon cayenne
½ teaspoon ground black pepper

1 flat or center-cut beef brisket (5 to 6 pounds), trimmed, with ¼ inch to ½ inch fat on one side

BEER MOP

1½ cups beer
¾ cup apple cider
¼ cup cider vinegar
¼ cup vegetable oil
¼ cup Worcestershire sauce
2 tablespoons Tabasco

3 cups Rich and Smoky Texas Barbecue Sauce (page 115)
or your favorite barbecue sauce
6 cups wood chips (hickory)

BEFORE YOU GO: Make the barbecue sauce (or plan to bring your own). The night before, mix spice rub ingredients in small bowl. Put 1 tablespoon of rub in large freezer-weight zipper-lock bag and set aside. Scatter remaining spice rub evenly over brisket and put brisket in 2-gallon freezer-weight zipper-lock bag. Seal and chill in refrigerator or cooler overnight.

Mix mop ingredients into bag with reserved spices. Seal and chill in refrigerator or cooler overnight.

The morning of the tailgate, put wood chips and enough cold water to cover in freezer-weight zipper-lock bags. Seal and chill in cooler for 1 hour. Or if your cooler's full, soak the chips at the game in a bag or bucket.

WHEN YOU GET THERE: Remove brisket from cooler about 20 minutes before grilling. Heat grill to medium-low (300° to 325°F). If using charcoal, spread hot coals to opposite sides, and drop a large disposable aluminum drip pan in empty space in middle. Brush and oil grill rack. Drain about 1 cup wood chips and scatter ½ cup over coals on each side. If using gas, drain all of wood chips and put in smoker box or in foil directly over one of the heated burners (see page 28). Heat gas grill to high until you see lots of smoke, then turn heat to medium-low. Turn off middle burner(s), or if you only have two burners, turn off the burner that doesn't have the wood chips over it.

Put brisket, fatty side up, over unheated part of grill (over drip pan). Cover and cook until severely browned and blackened in spots or very well done, 5 to 6 hours (about 190°F on an instant-read thermometer). If using charcoal, add fresh coals and remaining wood chips when the old ones die out, about once an hour. Mop or drizzle brisket with beer mixture on both sides whenever surface looks dry, every 40 to 60 minutes. Let rest 20 minutes off the heat.

Trim excess fat and slice across grain (don't trim too much—the crispy bits taste incredibly good). Serve with barbecue sauce. Brisket will stay warm for an hour or two, especially if loosely covered with foil.

NEIGHBORLY TIPS If you really need to speed up the cooking for some reason (hungry fans, cops kicking you out of the parking lot), it can be done. After about 2 hours of naked barbecuing, wrap the brisket in a couple layers of foil and raise the grill's heat to medium (about 325°F). Continue cooking over indirect heat for another 1 to 2 hours, or until the meat is well done, about 175°F on an instant-read thermometer. Then slather on your barbecue sauce, fold up the foil, and continue cooking until very well done, 180° to 190°F, about another 30 minutes. You'll miss out on some deep smoke flavor this way, but at least your brisket will be cooked.

If you use your own barbecue sauce, don't make it overly sweet like a Kansas City sauce would be. It should be a little leaner and meaner with more cider vinegar and chile pepper. You could doctor up your favorite bottled BBQ sauce by stirring extra cider vinegar and Tabasco into it.

Buffalo Chicken Wings

Chicken wings are standard fare at Ralph Wilson Stadium, home of the Buffalo Bills. The city of Buffalo made the culinary history books in 1964 when Teressa Bellissimo put her unique spin on chicken wings, which are often considered a throwaway part of the bird. She used up extra wings by deep-frying them and serving them with melted butter and hot sauce. Blue cheese dressing on the side completed the now famous combo known as Buffalo wings or simply "hot wings." For my taste, wings on the grill are just as good as (if not better than) wings that are fried. I was explaining this to my cousin Terry Hoyt, a Philadelphia Eagles fan, and developed this recipe to prove it to him. Terry, can you doubt it now? These are damn fine wings. **MAKES 6 TO 8 SERVINGS**

WINGS AND SAUCE

4 pounds chicken wings, about 16 whole wings

3 tablespoons olive oil

Juice of ½ lemon

2 large garlic cloves, minced

1⅓ cups mild hot-pepper sauce

½ teaspoon salt

¼ teaspoon ground black pepper

12 tablespoons (1½ sticks) butter

BLUE CHEESE DRESSING

¾ cup sour cream

¾ cup mayonnaise

2 tablespoons minced onion

1 small garlic clove, minced

1 tablespoon white wine vinegar

½ teaspoon salt

¼ teaspoon ground black pepper

1 cup crumbled blue cheese

3 celery sticks, trimmed and cut crosswise into thirds, optional

BEFORE YOU GO: The night before, cut off and discard wing tips. Cut wings into two pieces through the joint. Mix oil, lemon juice, garlic, ⅓ cup of the hot sauce, ¼ teaspoon of the salt, and the pepper in 2-gallon freezer-weight zipper lock bag (or two smaller bags). Drop in wings, seal, and chill in refrigerator or cooler overnight.

Make the dressing by stirring together all ingredients in medium bowl. Chill in refrigerator or cooler. Bring butter, remaining hot sauce, remaining salt, and celery sticks, if using, with you.

WHEN YOU GET THERE: Remove wings and dressing from cooler about 20 minutes before grilling. Heat grill to medium and let rack get good and hot. Brush and oil rack, then grill wings until well browned all over and no longer pink in center near bones, 5 to 8 minutes per side.

Meanwhile, melt butter, remaining 1 cup hot sauce, and remaining ¼ teaspoon salt in large disposable aluminum pan on side of grill (or over a separate burner). If pan is small, pour half of sauce into another aluminum pan. Toss wings with sauce in pans; or, if you don't mind dirtying a bowl, put the wing sauce in a big bowl and toss with wings until fully coated. Serve warm with dressing and celery sticks, if using.

NEIGHBORLY TIPS To get the sauce right, use a mild hot-pepper sauce like Crystal Hot Sauce or Frank's Original Red Hot Cayenne Pepper Sauce. You can add a lot of these sauces without the spiciness going over the top. If you want more heat, add your favorite hot sauce to your heart's content.

If you're pressed for time, replace the dressing with store-bought bottled blue cheese dressing.

Keep a spray bottle of water at the grill to douse any flare-ups. Chicken skin tends to drip quite a bit of fat.

Chicken Spiedies

When my wife and I lived in Binghamton, New York, a hot-air balloon once landed in our backyard. The annual Spiedie and Balloon Festival lofted dozens of colorful hot-air balloons into the sky. But spiedies (pronounced SPEE-dees) were the original attraction at this festival. These sandwiches of marinated and grilled meat were a local specialty in and around Binghamton. According to Broome County locals, the sandwich was first served in 1939 at Augustino Iacovelli's restaurant in Endicott. The term "spiedie" probably comes from the Italian "spiedo", or kitchen spit, on which the meat was originally grilled. These sandwiches have since developed such a cult following that some fans have bottles of local spiedie marinade shipped all over the country. But spiedie marinade is little more than Italian vinaigrette. So I make it at home. Try using different vinegars, like red wine or balsamic vinegar. I use white wine vinegar so the chicken stays light colored while marinating. Either way, this makes a quick and easy (and tasty) sandwich from the grill. **MAKES 6 TO 8 SERVINGS**

2½ to 3 pounds boneless, skinless chicken breast

1 cup extra virgin olive oil

Juice of 2 lemons

3 tablespoons white wine vinegar

6 bay leaves, finely crumbled or chopped

6 large garlic cloves, minced

1 tablespoon salt

1 tablespoon dried oregano

2 teaspoons dried basil

2 teaspoons dried thyme

1 teaspoon ground black pepper

6 to 8 steak sandwich rolls

BEFORE YOU GO: Two nights before, cut the chicken into 1½-inch cubes. Whisk everything else but steak rolls in large freezer-weight zipper-lock bag until blended. Pour ¼ cup of marinade into small zipper-lock bag and chill in refrigerator or cooler. Drop chicken into bigger bag, seal, and marinate in refrigerator. If necessary to "melt" the olive oil (which can solidify in the fridge), remove chicken bag from fridge a couple times a day. Shake bag to redistribute marinade and return to fridge or cooler. Chicken will look white from acidity of marinade; this is normal and helps to tenderize the meat.

WHEN YOU GET THERE: Remove chicken and bag of reserved marinade from cooler 20 minutes before grilling. Heat grill to medium-high and let rack get good and hot. Brush and oil rack, then grill chicken pieces until nicely browned in spots and no longer pink in center, 8 to 10 minutes, turning often and drizzling with marinade from larger bag during first 5 to 7 minutes. Avoid overcooking; the chicken should be very moist and register about 160°F on an instant-read thermometer.

Warm steak rolls on side of grill, then brush or drizzle on reserved marinade. Put chicken into rolls and chomp down.

NEIGHBORLY TIPS Use an herby bottled Italian salad dressing as a quick substitute for the marinade.

Spiedies were originally made with lamb like a shish kebab. Try replacing the chicken with 2 pounds boneless lamb shoulder cut into 2-inch cubes. Add 2 tablespoons fresh mint (or 1 teaspoon dried) to the marinade. Or use other cubed meats like pork, beef, or venison.

While you're at the grill, toss on some onions, peppers, and mushrooms to serve in the spiedies. Mayonnaise makes a nice spread for the rolls. Some folks like a slice or two of cheese.

One enterprising spiedie seller now ships cubes of marinated and frozen spiedie meat to customers. If you want a no-sweat way to try spiedies, check out www.spiedies.com and grill the meat as directed above.

Some spiedie makers insist that the meat be skewered, put into the bun, then pulled off the skewer. I prefer to skip the skewering step and toss the chicken pieces right onto the grill.

Barbecued Chicken

It seems so simple, but barbecued chicken often comes off the grill burnt, dried out, and thoroughly unsatisfying. Don't waste a good bird. Keep three things in mind: 1) Marinate the bird to keep it moist and flavorful. 2) Keep the heat low or use indirect heat. 3) Baste with barbecue sauce only at the end so the sauce doesn't burn. To keep things simple, I use Italian salad dressing as a marinade here. A quick spice rub adds extra flavor. And the finishing sauce is a basic sweet and smoky barbecue sauce. **MAKES 4 SERVINGS**

1 bottle (24 ounces) Italian salad dressing, about 3 cups

3½ to 4 pounds bone-in chicken breasts, thighs, and drumsticks

1 tablespoon salt

1 tablespoon light brown sugar

1 tablespoon sweet paprika

1 teaspoon ground black pepper

1 teaspoon dry mustard

½ teaspoon garlic powder

½ teaspoon onion powder

2 cups Sweet and Smoky Barbecue Sauce (page 115) or your favorite jarred barbecue sauce

2 cups wood chips or chunks (hickory or oak)

BEFORE YOU GO: Make the barbecue sauce (or plan to bring your own). The morning of the tailgate, pour dressing into a 2-gallon freezer-weight zipper-lock bag or divide between two 1-gallon bags. Drop in chicken pieces, seal, and chill in cooler.

Mix everything else but wood chips and barbecue sauce in small zipper-lock bag. Seal and stash in carry-all bag or cooler.

Put wood chips and enough cold water to cover in freezer-weight zipper-lock bag. Seal and chill in cooler for 1 hour. Or if your cooler's full, soak the chips at the game in a bag or bucket.

WHEN YOU GET THERE: Remove chicken from cooler about 20 minutes before grilling. Put chicken pieces on cutting board and discard marinade. Scatter spice rub all over chicken.

Heat grill to medium. If using charcoal, spread hot coals to opposite sides, leaving a large unheated space in middle. Brush and oil grill rack. Drain about 1 cup wood chips and scatter ½ cup over coals on each side. If using gas, drain all of wood chips and put in smoker box or in foil directly over one of the heated burners (see page 28). Heat gas grill to high until you see lots of smoke, then turn heat to medium-low. Turn off middle burner(s), or if you only have two burners, turn off the burner that doesn't have the wood chips over it.

Put chicken, skin side up, over unheated part of grill. Cover and cook, without turning, until chicken is no longer pink and juices run clear (about 170°F for breasts and 180°F for thighs on an instant-read thermometer inserted into thickest part without touching bone), 30 to 40 minutes total. Breasts cook faster, so check them first. During the last 5 minutes of grilling, baste chicken with barbecue sauce and move over the heated part of grill to brown all over. Serve with remaining barbecue sauce.

NEIGHBORLY TIPS You can serve all of the barbecue sauce on the side if you like and just cook the chicken until it's done without brushing with sauce.

You could skip the spice mix and just use barbecue sauce. I like the added flavor of the spice mix with just a little barbecue sauce.

One of my favorite bottled Italian dressings is Ken's Steakhouse Northern Italian, which also comes in a lower-calorie version.

Jerk Chicken

Originating in Jamaica, this spicy chicken is slow-grilled with lots of wood smoke, a barbecue method that results in really flavorful meat. If you're a chile-lover, you probably know all about Scotch bonnets. They are one of the hottest peppers on the planet, clocking in at 300,000 Scoville units, the scientific measurement of a chile pepper's heat level. Scotch bonnets also come packed with a heady mix of floral tropical aromas. If you can't find this chile, use its close relative, habanero chile peppers. Three peppers will make this recipe hot, but edible by most folks. If you've got card-carrying chileheads at the tailgate, add more chiles to taste. It's definitely worth starting the recipe the night before for the least hassle and most flavor. **MAKES 4 SERVINGS**

JERK PASTE

10 scallions, roots trimmed, coarsely chopped

3 to 10 Scotch bonnet chiles, seeded and coarsely chopped

3 garlic cloves, chopped

2 tablespoons chopped fresh ginger

⅓ cup fresh thyme

⅓ cup packed dark brown sugar

2 teaspoons allspice

1 teaspoon cinnamon

1 teaspoon nutmeg

1 teaspoon ground coriander

1 teaspoon salt

1 teaspoon ground black pepper

¼ cup vegetable oil

2 tablespoons soy sauce

2 tablespoons lime juice

1 tablespoon dark rum

CHICKEN

2 tablespoons vegetable oil

3½ to 4 pounds bone-in chicken breasts, thighs, and drumsticks

2 cups wood chips or chunks (hickory or oak)

BEFORE YOU GO: Put jerk paste ingredients in food processor. Process to loose paste, about 30 seconds. Scrape down sides of processor bowl if necessary. Taste and add more chile peppers or other spices as necessary. Use immediately or refrigerate in an airtight container for up to 1 month (if you really want to get a head start on your tailgate!).

When ready to make the chicken, set aside about ¾ cup paste and pour into a small zipper-lock bag. Stir in vegetable oil, seal, and store in refrigerator or cooler. Divide the remaining jerk paste between two large freezer-weight zipper-lock bags. Drop chicken breasts into one bag and thighs and drumsticks into the other. Press air out of the bags, seal, and massage paste into chicken until completely coated. Store in refrigerator or cooler for at least 3 hours or overnight.

The morning of the tailgate, put wood chips and enough cold water to cover in freezer-weight zipper-lock bag. Seal and chill in cooler for 1 hour. Or if your cooler's full, soak the chips at the game in a bag or bucket.

WHEN YOU GET THERE: Remove chicken and reserved jerk paste from cooler about 20 minutes before grilling. Heat grill to medium. If using charcoal, spread hot coals to opposite sides, leaving a large unheated space in middle. Brush and oil grill rack. Drain about 1 cup wood chips and scatter ½ cup over coals on each side. If using gas, drain all of wood chips and put in smoker box or in foil directly over one of the heated burners (see page 28). Heat gas grill to high until you see lots of smoke, then turn heat to medium-low. Turn off middle burner(s), or if you only have two burners, turn off the burner that doesn't have the wood chips over it.

Put chicken, skin side up, over unheated part of grill. Cover and cook, without turning, until chicken is no longer pink and juices run clear (about 170°F for breasts and 180°F for thighs on an instant-read thermometer inserted into thickest portion without touching bone), 30 to 40 minutes total. Breasts cook faster, so check them first. Use basting brush to dab chicken with reserved jerk paste every 10 minutes or so.

NEIGHBORLY TIP The most tedious part of this recipe is stripping the fresh thyme leaves from their stems. To rush it, replace the ⅓ cup fresh thyme with 2 tablespoons dried thyme.

Beer-Butt Chicken

If you haven't grilled chicken on a beer can yet, what are you waiting for? Your tail-gating buddies will no doubt be impressed when a whole chicken impaled on a can of beer comes off your grill beautifully brown and meltingly moist. It's an ingeniously simple method, as long as you don't spill the beer (but that's always the rule with beer). Here's a basic version. Feel free to experiment with different spice rubs and even types of canned liquids. Soda, tomato juice, or just about any liquid that can steam in the can will lend its moisture and subtle flavor to the bird. For the ultimate in flavor variations, check out Steven Raichlen's entire book on the subject, aptly named Beer-Can Chicken. **MAKES ABOUT 4 SERVINGS**

2 tablespoons paprika

1 tablespoon dark brown sugar

1 tablespoon salt

1 teaspoon cayenne

1 teaspoon dry mustard

½ teaspoon garlic powder

½ teaspoon onion powder

½ teaspoon ground black pepper

1 chicken, about 4 pounds

1 can (12 ounces) beer

2 cups wood chips (preferably hickory or oak), optional

BEFORE YOU GO: The morning of the tailgate, mix everything but chicken, beer, and wood chips in small zipper-lock bag. Remove giblets and fat from inside of chicken. Rinse chicken inside and out and pat dry with paper towels. Rub about a teaspoon of spice mix inside chicken. Coat outside of chicken with cooking spray (or brush with oil), then rub all over with spice mix, especially under legs and wings. Save about 1 tablespoon spice mix in bag. Seal the bag and stash in your carry-all or cooler. Put rubbed chicken in 2-gallon freezer-weight zipper-lock bag. Seal and chill in refrigerator or cooler.

Put wood chips, if using, and enough cold water to cover in freezer-weight zipper-lock bag. Seal and chill in cooler for 1 hour. Or if your cooler's full, soak the chips at the game in a bag or bucket.

WHEN YOU GET THERE: Remove chicken from cooler about 20 minutes before grilling. Put chicken on cutting board and scatter remaining spice rub onto any bare spots on chicken. Drink half the beer. Or find a half-empty beer around your tailgate. If you have an old-fashioned pointy can opener, pop a few extra holes in the top of the can to help spread out the steam. Hold chicken upright with its butt down and slide it over beer can until nice and snug. Tuck wings behind the bird's back. Prop legs forward to make a tripod so chicken sits stably on the board. This is how the bird will sit on the grill.

Heat grill to medium. If using charcoal, spread hot coals to opposite sides, leaving a large unheated space in middle. Brush and oil grill rack. Drain about 1 cup wood chips and scatter ½ cup over coals on each side. If using gas, drain all of wood chips and put in smoker box or in foil directly over one of the heated burners (see page 28). Heat gas grill to high until you see lots of smoke, then turn heat to medium-low. Turn off middle burner(s), or if you only have two burners, turn off the burner that doesn't have the wood chips over it.

Put chicken and beer can over unheated part of grill, pulling legs forward so it sits stably on the grill rack. Cover and cook until skin is brown and crisp and juices run clear, about 180°F on an instant-read thermometer inserted into thick part of thigh (without touching bone). Total time should be 1¼ to 1½ hours. If using charcoal, add more hot coals when old ones burn out, after about 45 minutes. Using big tongs and silicone gloves or insulated grill mitts, carefully transfer chicken and can onto platter or cutting board. Let rest 5 minutes on the can. Lift bird off can and onto cutting board. Carve and serve.

NEIGHBORLY TIPS For 8 servings, grill two birds at once. If you're using a standard 21-inch Weber kettle grill, you should be able to fit two 3½-pound birds at once on the center of the grill. Double the recipe and add 10 to 15 minutes cooking time. If the birds start to brown too much before the meat is cooked, loosely cover them with foil.

Heatproof silicone gloves are great for lifting whole birds and big pieces of hot meat off the grill. Most are waterproof, heatproof, and hot-oil-proof. You can even grab hot coals with them. They withstand temperatures up to 500°F and are dishwasher safe. Need I say more? There are a few consumer brands available, such as Orka and Dolphin, as well as commercial brands, with which you can safely grab a whole chicken right off the grill. Look for silicone gloves at your local cookware store or check the sources beginning on page 182.

Chipotle-Lime Shrimp with Grilled Salsa

When you've got extra plum tomatoes on hand, try this fast and fancy appetizer. You can serve it hot off the grill, at room temperature, or chilled. **MAKES 4 SERVINGS**

6 large plum tomatoes, cored and halved crosswise

1 lime

¼ cup olive oil

1 teaspoon chipotle powder

½ teaspoon salt

1 pound shrimp, peeled and deveined, thawed if frozen

½ red bell pepper, seeded and cut in half

2 slices onion, each ½ inch thick

4 large garlic cloves, unpeeled

¼ cup chopped fresh cilantro

BEFORE YOU GO: Dig a knife tip or your fingers into cut sides of tomatoes to remove seeds and pulp. Zest the lime and put zest in large freezer-weight zipper-lock bag. Squeeze juice from half the lime into bag. Mix in oil, chipotle powder, and salt. Pour 2 tablespoons of marinade into another large zipper-lock bag. Drop shrimp in second bag, seal, and chill in cooler up to 1 hour. Drop tomatoes and pepper pieces into first bag and massage marinade into crevices. Slip in onion slices and gently turn to coat. Seal bag and chill in cooler up to 1 hour. (If you'll be traveling more than 1 hour, do this prep at the tailgate.)

WHEN YOU GET THERE: Remove shrimp and vegetables from cooler 20 minutes before grilling. Heat grill to medium-high and let rack get good and hot. Thread unpeeled cloves of garlic and marinated shrimp onto separate skewers. Discard shrimp marinade.

Brush and oil rack, then grill everything until nicely grill marked all over, 3 to 5 minutes per side (shrimp should be bright pink and firm; vegetables should be tender). Reserve remaining marinade in vegetable bag.

Remove grilled vegetables to a cutting board and chop. Squeeze garlic from skins and chop. Put vegetables and garlic back into vegetable bag with reserved marinade and 2 tablespoons of cilantro. Seal and turn to mix.

Put grilled shrimp on platter or plates with grilled vegetable salsa. Garnish with remaining cilantro.

NEIGHBORLY TIP Chipotles are smoke-dried jalapeño chiles. Most grocery stores carry ground chipotle powder in the "gourmet" spice aisle. Use it as you would cayenne pepper, which means sparingly. It's got quite a kick!

Texas Stadium Opens Religiously

The first event held at Texas Stadium, home of the Dallas Cowboys, wasn't a tailgate. No, it wasn't a dance by the team's famed cheerleaders. Hell, it wasn't even a football game.

It was a rally for evangelist Billy Graham. Later that year, on October 24, 1971, the Cowboys finally entered their new home and beat the New England Patriots 44–21.

Beer Boiled Shrimp

Talk about your easy appetizers. This one's effortless. Okay, you do have to chop some garlic and parsley. For this one iota of exertion, you get rewarded with drinking half a can of beer as part of the recipe. **MAKES 4 SERVINGS**

Half a 12-ounce can beer

Juice of ½ lemon

4 garlic cloves, minced

3 tablespoons chopped fresh parsley

1 tablespoon crab boil seasoning, such as Old Bay

1 pound medium shrimp, peeled and deveined, tails removed (thawed if frozen)

3 tablespoons butter

BEFORE YOU GO: The morning of the tailgate, mix everything but the shrimp and butter in large freezer-weight zipper-lock bag. Drop in shrimp, seal, and chill in cooler. Drink the rest of the beer. Or dump it. (No! Don't waste good beer!)

WHEN YOU GET THERE: Heat grill to medium-high and let rack get good and hot. Pour shrimp and marinade into a small disposable aluminum pan. Or make a pan out of a foot-long sheet of heavy-duty foil. Add butter to shrimp and cover pan with foil or crimp the top shut on your makeshift pan. Put pan on grill rack and grill until shrimp are bright pink, 5 to 10 minutes, shaking the pan and poking the shrimp with tongs a couple times. Serve immediately with toothpicks for casual eats. Or serve over rice all nice and proper-like. Or, hell, make a sandwich: grab a hot dog bun, throw on a few shrimp and some juices, and chow down.

NEIGHBORLY TIPS For Spicy Beer Boiled Shrimp, add ¼ teaspoon cayenne along with the Old Bay.

Use a cutting board or cookie sheet to transfer a makeshift foil pan to and from the grill rack.

When eating these, spoon up some juices and garlic bits from the bottom of the pan for more flavor.

Tales Behind the Teams

Some NFL teams are named after animals that could tear you apart, such as Panthers and Jaguars. Others have a more curious history.

- Kansas City Chiefs. Forget any notion of the team being named after a brave tribe of warriors hailing from America's frontier. The Chiefs were named after Kansas City mayor H. Roe "Chief" Bartle, who is also the namesake of a vast hall in a local convention center.

- Miami Dolphins. The sea is filled with animals such as sharks that would make good football mascots. So why the Dolphins? In 1965, the team chose this gentle creature after receiving nearly twenty thousand entries in a naming contest. Mrs. Robert Swanson won two lifetime passes to Dolphins games for her brilliant suggestion. She explained that the creatures are fast and smart.

- Green Bay Packers. So what is a packer, anyway? Someone stuffing a suitcase for vacation? Actually, the Indian Packing Company employed the team's founder and coach, Curly Lambeau, and provided the players with jerseys and a practice field. The company was bought out by other meatpacking companies and is now long gone, but the team carries on its legacy. Curly Lambeau's gone, too, but the stadium that the Packers play in carries his name.

- Oakland Raiders. This California team was almost named the Oakland Señors. Can you imagine what the team symbol would have been? Thank God for the genius who approved the Oakland Raiders instead. The Raiders now have one of the most intimidating emblems in the NFL: a silver and black shield with two crossed swords and pirate.

- Baltimore Ravens. Maryland's team was named after Edgar Allan Poe's famous poem "The Raven." Poe lived for a time in Baltimore and died there under mysterious circumstances, possibly of rabies, alcohol abuse, or carbon monoxide poisoning. Poe himself was small and frail, but his haunting poem with its talking raven has frightened people for more than 150 years.

Maple-Rosemary Planked Salmon

The flavors here are redolent of the mountainous northern American coasts, both east and west. Pine-scented rosemary...thickly sweet maple syrup...buttery soft salmon. These grilled fillets would be perfectly at home before a New England Patriots or Seattle Seahawks game. To simplify grilling the fillet and enhance the woodsy flavors, I use the time-honored method of cooking the salmon on a plank of cedar. Gourmet kitchen shops and supermarkets often carry these (see mail-order sources beginning on page 182). Or you can buy untreated cedar shingles at a home store or lumberyard. Any untreated 1/4-inch-thick plank of cedar or alder wood will do. But never use treated wood when cooking. That's a recipe for disaster. **MAKES 6 SERVINGS**

1 cedar or alder plank, about 6 × 12 × 1/4 inches

3 tablespoons pure maple syrup

2 tablespoons extra virgin olive oil

2 tablespoons tamari or soy sauce

2 tablespoons chopped fresh rosemary, plus 2 sprigs for garnish

1 teaspoon toasted sesame oil

3 garlic cloves, minced

Zest of 1 lemon

1/4 teaspoon salt

1/4 teaspoon ground black pepper

1 salmon fillet (about 2 pounds), bones removed

6 lemon wedges

BEFORE YOU GO: The morning of the tailgate, put wood plank in 2-gallon freezer-weight zipper-lock bag or other big, strong plastic bag. Cover with water, seal, and chill in cooler 2 to 10 hours.

Mix everything else but the fish and lemon in a 2-gallon freezer-weight zipper-lock bag. Slip fish, skin side up, into bag of marinade. Seal and chill in cooler 1 to 4 hours.

WHEN YOU GET THERE: Heat grill to medium-high and let rack get good and hot. Drain wood plank. Remove fish from marinade and put skin side down on plank. Brush and oil rack, then put planked fish in center and lay rosemary sprigs over fish. Cover and grill until fish is just a bit filmy and moist in the middle (about 140°F on an instant-read thermometer), 10 to 15 minutes. Move plank to a heat-proof surface or cutting board. Cut fish crosswise into 6 pieces. Pass lemon wedges for squeezing on top.

NEIGHBORLY TIPS You can use salmon fillets with or without skin. If there's no skin, brush the bottom of the fillet with oil before putting on the plank. Either way, check to make sure all the bones are removed before marinating the fish. Lay the fillet skin side down and run your fingers down the flesh in both directions, feeling for tiny bones. Pull out any bones with clean needlenose pliers or tweezers.

It's easiest to zest a lemon for the marinade, then bring along the same naked lemon and cut it into wedges for squeezing.

Corn Trivia

The next time you're chewing through ears of grilled corn with your buddies, share some corn facts with them (check your teeth first—no one looks smart with those kernels between their choppers).

- An ear of corn always has an even number of rows of kernels.

- A typical ear of field corn contains 600 to 800 kernels.

- Corn reproduces a little bit like humans, but with a G rating. Each corn plant has both male and female parts (okay, this part isn't like most humans). The male parts release millions of grains of pollen. The silks—the fine hairlike structures you later peel away from your ear of corn—each grab one grain of pollen. This grain makes its way down a tube inside the silk to a structure called an *ovule*. When ovule and pollen meet, you get a kernel of corn.

- The military rank "colonel" has a corny pronunciation but has nothing to do with the vegetable. It started with the Italian *colonello* and migrated to the French *coronel*. The British picked it up and spelled it like the Italians and pronounced it like the French. Go figure.

Swordfish Steaks with Pineapple Relish

Serve these quick fish steaks during warm weather or rainy tailgates. They grill up in about 10 minutes, so you spend less time over the grill. The bright-flavored tropical salsa also lightens things up. **MAKES 4 SERVINGS**

1 can (20 ounces) pineapple slices, undrained

1 kiwi, peeled and finely chopped

¼ cup finely chopped red onion

1 small jalapeño chile, seeded and finely chopped

1 tablespoon fresh lime juice

1 tablespoon chopped fresh cilantro

4 swordfish steaks (1½ to 2 pounds total, each 1 inch thick)

½ teaspoon salt

⅛ teaspoon ground black pepper

WHEN YOU GET THERE: Heat grill to medium-high and let rack get good and hot. Drain pineapple, reserving juice. Brush and oil rack, then grill pineapple until nicely grill marked, 3 to 5 minutes per side. Chop into bite-size chunks and place in medium bowl. Stir in kiwi, onion, jalapeño, lime juice, cilantro, and 1 tablespoon of reserved juice. Cover and set aside for 15 to 20 minutes to blend flavors.

Coat swordfish all over with oil or cooking spray. Sprinkle with salt and pepper. Grill over medium heat until fish is just a bit filmy and moist in the middle, 4 to 6 minutes per side. Serve with pineapple relish.

NEIGHBORLY TIPS For the best flavor, use fresh pineapple instead of canned. Cut off the spiky top and base from a small pineapple (about 2½ pounds). Cut the fruit lengthwise into quarters. Slice out the tough woody core from each quarter. Sit each quarter rind side down on the cutting board and run the knife as close to the rind as possible, cutting the fruit away from the rind. Slice the fruit crosswise into wedges, then grill as directed. Add 1 tablespoon of the accumulated juices to the relish.

To seed and chop a jalapeño chile without touching the hot capsaicin (the stuff that gives chiles their heat), hold the chile by the stem using your fingertips. Cut off ⅛ inch from the tip then stand the chile on the flattened tip. Still holding the stem, slice downward from stem to tip, removing the flesh from the core in sections. Discard the stem, core, and seeds. To chop, slice the flesh lengthwise, then crosswise, steadying the flesh with another small knife or other utensil.

Patriot Zip's View of Tailgating

Randy Pierce doesn't let a little adversity stand in the way of enjoying his beloved New England Patriots. He just gets by with a little help from his friends.

Known to the New England Patriots fan community as "Patriot Zip," Pierce became legally blind in 1989 because of a progressive condition, and has been completely without sight since 2000. The Nashua, New Hampshire, resident still holds season tickets to the games, though, and brings a different friend to each game. The Patriots experience then turns into a collaborative effort: the friend drives to the game and supplies food and drink, and Zip provides the tickets and the tailgating equipment.

Zip, the 2001 Patriots Fan of the Year, usually brings to the games a canopy shelter that he walls off for cold-weather tailgating and a couple grills for cooking and providing heat. But before one Jets-Patriots rivalry game, Zip had recently broken his right leg and left wrist, which coupled with his blindness made getting to the game and setting up his tailgate area "tough," he says with some understatement.

In true tailgating spirit, the proprietor of a popular Jets fan Web site arrived early that day with his tailgating crew and sat in Zip's customary spot to save it until the banged-up Patriots fan finally arrived.

"For me, that's what it's all about," Zip says. "That's probably my top tailgating memory."

Miami Dolphinfish Steaks

Dolphinfish, also known as mahi mahi or dorado, is a great fish to grill when your team is playing the Miami Dolphins. Grill the opposition! Then eat 'em! Here, the mild flavor of this dark-fleshed fish gets a Caribbean shot of flavor with a marinade of orange, lime, rum, and scallions. Mango-orange salsa livens things up even more. One-Two Punch (page 143) would be the perfect drink. **MAKES 4 SERVINGS**

2 navel oranges

1 lime

3 tablespoons extra virgin olive oil

1 tablespoon (½ ounce) dark or spiced rum

3 scallions (green and white parts), finely chopped

½ teaspoon salt

¼ teaspoon ground black pepper

4 mahi mahi steaks (each about 8 ounces and 1½ inches thick)

1 mango, pitted, peeled, and finely chopped (see Tips)

1 large California red (Fresno) or red jalapeño chile, seeded and finely chopped

2 teaspoons finely minced or grated fresh ginger

1 tablespoon chopped fresh cilantro

BEFORE YOU GO: The morning of the tailgate, juice half an orange and half a lime into a large freezer-weight zipper-lock bag. Mix in olive oil, rum, two of the scallions, ¼ teaspoon of the salt, and the pepper. Drop in fish steaks, seal, and chill in cooler for up to 2 hours. (If it will be longer than 2 hours before you get there, pack the fish separately in the cooler and marinate for 1 hour when you get there. The rest of the prep can be done ahead.)

Peel remaining orange and half orange and trim off bitter white membrane from flesh. Coarsely chop flesh and scrape flesh and any juices into large freezer-weight zipper-lock bag. Juice remaining half lime into bag. Gently mix in mango, chile, ginger, cilantro, remaining scallion, and remaining ¼ teaspoon salt. Seal and chill in cooler.

WHEN YOU GET THERE: Remove fish and mango-orange salsa from cooler 20 minutes before grilling. Heat grill to medium-low and let rack get good and hot. Brush and oil rack, then grill fish until nicely browned outside and just a little filmy and moist in the middle, 4 to 5 minutes per side, brushing with marinade from bag. Serve with salsa.

NEIGHBORLY TIPS If you can't find steaks, use 4 mahi mahi fillets (about 7 ounces each and ¾ inch thick). Use a fish grilling basket to turn the fillets easily. Look for these cheap contraptions in hardware stores or cookware stores. You could also replace the mahi mahi with swordfish steaks.

To peel, pit, and chop a mango, stand it upright on a cutting board. Cut down through the flesh on one of the flatter sides, guiding the knife as close around the oval-shaped pit as possible. Repeat on the other side to make two disks of fruit, plus a third centerpiece with the pit. Cut the peel off the center piece, then cut the fruit off the pit, discarding pit and peels. Hold one of the disks in your hand and use your knife to score the flesh all the way down to the peel in a checkerboard pattern (without cutting through the peel and into your hand). Push up through the peel side of the disk to expose the cubes of flesh. Cut the flesh away from the peel and discard the peel. Repeat with the other disk.

- -

Grilled Stuffed French Toast

Now, here's how to kick off a tailgating party in style—with grilled breakfast! The whole thing is assembled the night before, so all you have to do is put the soaked bread on the grill. Don't forget the maple syrup. **MAKES 4 SERVINGS**

1 loaf (about 1 pound) Italian bread

8 ounces cream cheese, at room temperature

3 tablespoons confectioners' sugar

½ teaspoon almond extract

½ cup seedless strawberry or raspberry preserves

5 large eggs

1½ cups light cream or half-and-half

1 teaspoon vanilla extract

Pinch of salt

BEFORE YOU GO: The night before, cut off and discard ends of bread. Cut bread into about eight 1½-inch-thick slices. Cut slit through top crust of each slice to form deep pocket.

Mix cream cheese, 2 tablespoons of the sugar, and the almond extract in medium bowl. Spread equally among bread pockets, then spoon preserves equally among pockets next to cream cheese. Lay stuffed bread in single layer in shallow 4-quart baking dish (such as 15 × 10-inch dish).

In clean medium bowl, mix eggs, cream or half-and-half, vanilla extract, salt, and remaining 1 tablespoon sugar. Pour evenly over bread. Tilt dish and swirl eggs to completely coat bread. Cover and chill in refrigerator or top of cooler overnight.

WHEN YOU GET THERE: Remove dish from cooler 20 minutes before grilling. Heat grill to medium and let rack get good and hot. Brush and oil rack, then grill French toast until nicely browned, about 5 minutes per side, flipping with spatula. Serve immediately.

NEIGHBORLY TIPS For a fancy glaze, mix together 2 tablespoons honey, 2 tablespoons grated orange zest, 3 tablespoons well softened butter, and ¼ teaspoon cinnamon. Brush this glaze over the hot French toast before serving. Makes it look and taste delish!

Try this recipe for dessert, too.

Be sure to brush your grill rack until scrupulously clean. Otherwise, your French toast may taste like your last grilled meal.

Bringing a Little Civility to War

The date was July 21, 1861, and a crowd of early tailgaters loaded up their picnic baskets and headed over to Manassas Junction, Virginia, from Washington, D.C.

The Blues were taking on the Grays in an early contest of what would be a long-running and decidedly unfriendly rivalry: the Civil War. Historians would later call this match the Battle of Bull Run. At the time, though, genteel ladies with their fancy gowns were just expecting an exciting picnic in the country, followed by delightful parties in town after the battle.

Instead, the Union forces, terrified by the startling new "rebel yell" the fiery Confederates unleashed, broke ranks and ran. The scene turned into a melee as soldiers and picnickers collided while trying to scramble away from the battlefield. Needless to say, a good time was had by none at this fledgling tailgate event. Fortunately, modern sports have evolved to keep the players and spectators fairly separated. Of course, the spectators still clash among themselves, but that's another story.

Grilled Pound Cake and Bananas Foster

Dessert on the grill? Absolutely! And this one's so easy, you can make the whole thing at the tailgate. You could cut the cake and make the sauce at home. But the sauce gets reheated at the game anyway. Look for yellow bananas that are barely spotted brown. They should be ripe yet firm. **MAKES 8 SERVINGS**

8 tablespoons (1 stick) unsalted butter

1½ cups packed dark brown sugar

½ cup dark rum

1 teaspoon cinnamon

1 pound cake (16 ounces)

4 firm ripe bananas

1 can (7 ounces) whipped cream

WHEN YOU GET THERE: Heat grill to medium-high and let rack get good and hot. Melt butter, brown sugar, rum, and cinnamon in small pan over medium-low heat until slightly thickened, 10 to 15 minutes. Cut pound cake into 8 slices, each 1 to 2 inches thick. Peel bananas and cut each crosswise in half to make a total of 8 pieces.

Brush pound cake slices and banana pieces with brown sugar mixture, saving about half of the sauce for serving.

Brush and oil grill rack, then grill bananas and cake on rack until bananas are nicely grill marked and cake is toasted, 2 to 4 minutes per side (bananas may take slightly longer depending upon ripeness).

Put cake on plates and top with bananas, cutting up bananas, if desired. Drizzle with extra sauce and squirt with whipped cream.

NEIGHBORLY TIPS If your bananas are very ripe, leave the peels on and cut the whole bananas in half lengthwise. Brush the cut side with sauce, then grill in the skins, cut side down, basting and turning as directed.

Be sure to brush your grill rack until it's clean. Nothing kills a good dessert like burnt beef flavor.

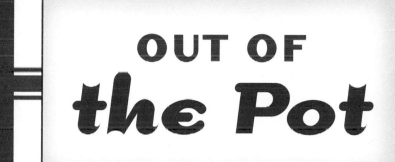

OUT OF
the Pot

Basic Barbecue Sauce

This recipe makes a sauce that's similar to—but sooooo much tastier than—popular bottled barbecue sauces. It takes just a few minutes to stir everything together, then you let it simmer on low heat a bit. I like to make a double batch of this recipe ahead of time, since it's used so often, as in Barbecue Beans (page 116), Chipotle-Bourbon Ribs (page 74), Barbecued Chicken (page 94), and Beer-Mopped Brisket with Texas Barbecue Sauce (page 88). It's so easy to put together, you could just make the sauce at the tailgate. And as long as you're making your own sauce, it's worth it to add the extras listed below. These flavors will make a sauce worthy of any food that comes off your grill. But if you need to take a cheap shortcut, buy your favorite bottled barbecue sauce and stir in the extras listed in the variations over low heat. **MAKES ABOUT 3 CUPS**

2 cups ketchup

3 tablespoons dark brown sugar

3 tablespoons cider vinegar

2 tablespoons yellow mustard

2 tablespoons Worcestershire sauce

2 teaspoons paprika

1½ teaspoons salt

1 teaspoon garlic powder

½ teaspoon onion powder

½ teaspoon ground black pepper

BEFORE YOU GO: Put everything in a medium saucepan and bring to a boil over high heat. Reduce the heat to medium-low and simmer for 20 minutes, or until slightly thickened. Cover and bring to the tailgate or chill in airtight container in refrigerator or cooler up to 1 month.

WHEN YOU GET THERE: Reheat sauce over low heat. Keep warm for brushing onto barbecued meats (cold sauce brushed onto hot meat lowers the meat temperature slightly and slows down the cooking).

NEIGHBORLY TIPS To vary the flavor, follow one or a combination of these variations.

Rich Barbecue Sauce: Add ¼ cup butter.

Sweet Barbecue Sauce: Add 2 tablespoons molasses and 1 tablespoon honey.

Smoky Barbecue Sauce: Add 2 teaspoons liquid smoke (available in the spice aisle of most grocery stores).

Sweet and Smoky Barbecue Sauce: Add 2 tablespoons molasses, 1 tablespoon honey, and 2 teaspoons liquid smoke.

Rich, Sweet, and Smoky Chipotle-Bourbon Barbecue Sauce: Add ¼ cup butter, 2 tablespoons molasses, 1 tablespoon honey, 2 teaspoons liquid smoke, 1 tablespoon chipotle powder, and ½ cup good-quality bourbon. (Look for chipotle powder in the spice aisle of your grocery store.)

Rich and Smoky Texas Barbecue Sauce: Up the cider vinegar to ½ cup and add ¼ cup butter, 2 teaspoons liquid smoke, 1 tablespoon pure chile powder (such as ancho), and 1 teaspoon cayenne pepper (or more to taste).

Barbecue Beans

Sure, you could buy baked beans in a can. But the texture of cooked dried beans is a lot less mushy. Plus, it's always more impressive when you bring something home-made. **MAKES 8 SERVINGS**

5 ounces dried navy beans or other small white beans, rinsed

5 ounces dried small pink beans, rinsed

4 ounces (about 4 slices) thick-cut sliced bacon, chopped

¾ cup chopped smoked ham

½ large onion, finely chopped

⅓ cup molasses

1¼ cups Sweet and Smoky Barbecue Sauce (page 115) or your favorite bottled barbecue sauce

½ teaspoon salt

¼ teaspoon ground black pepper

BEFORE YOU GO: Two nights before, put beans in large pot and cover with water by 2 inches. Let soak overnight.

Early the night before, drain beans in colander and set aside. Cook bacon in same bean pot over medium-low heat until crisp, about 10 minutes. Increase heat to medium, add ham and onion, and cook until onion softens, about 5 minutes. Add beans and enough hot water to cover beans by one inch (use hot tap water if your water is clean). Stir in molasses and barbecue sauce. Bring to a boil, then reduce heat to medium-low and simmer gently until beans are tender, 4 to 5 hours, stirring now and then and adding hot water as necessary. Stir in the salt and pepper, or more to taste. Cover and let sit overnight or chill in airtight container in refrigerator or cooler up to 1 week.

WHEN YOU GET THERE: Reheat beans over medium-low heat (on the grill if your pot handles can take it) until heated through.

NEIGHBORLY TIPS When rinsing beans, pick them over and remove any pebbles or old shriveled beans. Odd things sometimes end up in an otherwise good bag of beans.

To get a jump on the beans, make them up to a week ahead and keep them covered in the fridge. Reheat at the tailgate. Or do half the cooking at home and half when you get there.

Basic Tomato-Basil Sauce

You can make this sauce weeks in advance and freeze it. Use it for Meatball Hero (page 118) or as a dip for Grilled Calzones (page 66). Or just toss it with cooked pasta to feed those unexpected guests at your tailgate. **MAKES ABOUT 6 CUPS**

¼ cup extra virgin olive oil

1 onion, finely chopped

5 garlic cloves, minced

¼ cup tomato paste

1 cup dry red wine

2 cans (28 ounces each) plum tomatoes in puree

¼ cup chopped fresh basil or 2 teaspoons dried

1 teaspoon salt

½ teaspoon ground black pepper

BEFORE YOU GO: Heat 2 tablespoons of the oil in deep sauté pan over medium heat. When it's hot, add onion and cook until tender, about 5 minutes. Add garlic and cook 2 minutes. Stir in tomato paste. Add wine and cook until it reduces slightly in volume. Working near the pan, pluck tomatoes from can one by one. Grab the firm stem end of each tomato and pull out the core from the tomato flesh. Discard the core and tear the flesh with your hands, dropping tomato pieces into pan. Repeat with each tomato. Pour half of canning liquid into pan. Bring to boil, then reduce heat to medium-low and cook until tomatoes break down and thicken, about 45 minutes. Stir now and then and crush tomatoes with wooden spoon. Stir in remaining 2 tablespoons oil, basil, salt, and pepper. Taste and add more of any ingredient you think is lacking. Cool slightly and chill in airtight container in refrigerator or cooler up to 2 days. Or freeze up to 1 month.

WHEN YOU GET THERE: Reheat over medium-low heat until hot, about 10 minutes.

NEIGHBORLY TIPS For a smooth sauce, puree with a hand-held blender or in an upright blender or a food processor.

For a sausage sandwich, grill or fry your favorite sausages along with onions and peppers until cooked through. Serve on submarine rolls with Basic Tomato-Basil Sauce.

Meatball Hero

I look at this sandwich and think of hand-held spaghetti and meatballs. The hero roll stands in for the noodles, but other than that, it's the same: tender, tasty meat-balls served with the rich tomato sauce they simmered in. The perfect hot sandwich • *for a chilly day on the tarmac.* **MAKES 8 HEROS**

6 cups Basic Tomato-Basil Sauce (page 117) or your favorite tomato sauce

2 tablespoons olive oil

½ onion, minced

½ cup plain dried bread crumbs

½ cup half-and-half or whole milk

1 large egg, lightly beaten

½ cup chopped fresh parsley

2 pounds ground meat for meat loaf (beef, pork, and veal)

1 teaspoon salt

½ teaspoon ground black pepper

8 submarine sandwich rolls

BEFORE YOU GO: Make the Basic Tomato-Basil Sauce.

Heat oven to 375°F. Put oil in large rimmed baking sheet and heat in oven until oil is hot, 1 to 2 minutes. Stir onion into oil and roast until onion is tender, about 5 minutes, stirring now and then with stiff spatula.

Meanwhile, mix bread crumbs and half-and-half or milk in large bowl and let sit until milk is absorbed. Scrape cooked onions into same bowl along with egg, parsley, ground meat, salt, and pepper. Mix gently with your hands and shape into 1½-inch footballs or round meatballs. Put meatballs on baking sheet and roast until browned all over and no longer pink in center, 20 to 25 minutes, turning fre-quently (when done, meatballs will register about 160°F on an instant-read ther-mometer). Cool to room temperature and put in large zipper-lock bag. Seal and chill in refrigerator up to 2 days.

WHEN YOU GET THERE: Put meatballs in large saucepan and pour tomato sauce over top. Cook over medium-low heat until bubbly and meatballs are heated through, about 20 minutes. For each sandwich, put about 3 meatballs and some sauce on a roll.

NEIGHBORLY TIPS Put a couple slices of provolone on each roll before adding the meatballs and sauce. Or top with freshly shredded Parmesan.

Grocery stores and butchers often sell mixed ground meat for meat loaf and meatballs. I like these proportions: 60 percent beef, 20 percent pork, 20 percent veal.

The Ultimate Tailgating Truck

Some tailgaters make their entrance into the parking lot in customized school buses, RVs, and panel delivery trucks. Others simply toss their gear in the trunk of their car or truck bed.

Here's a nice balance between the two, a normal-looking vehicle that caters to a tail gater's dreams: Ford F150 Party Truck. This truck is customized by Galpin Motors in North Hills, California, and looks like a regular F150 truck on the outside. But when you flip up the tonneau cover and let down the tailgate, the party begins. The gear that slides out the back includes a grill, sink, blender, two beer taps, a flip-down DVD player, and a custom stereo. Up front, you'll find a leather interior and seating for six tailgaters. Buying this out-of-the-box tailgating luxury will set you back the better part of $70,000. But if this sounds like your kind of vehicle, cruise over to www.galpinized.com, or call 800-252-7207.

Beef on Weck

I wish I'd had one of these sandwiches the first time I visited Buffalo, New York. It was February and a blizzard was busy blanketing the city with snow. The outside temperature was −10°F with wind chill. No wonder this hot roast beef sandwich is the local specialty! The real specialty in the sandwich is its roll, known as kummel-weck and topped with a layer of crunchy caraway seeds and coarse salt. At Ralph Wilson Stadium, home of the Buffalo Bills, these sandwiches warm many a tailgater before the games. **MAKES 6 SANDWICHES**

6 Kaiser rolls

2 large eggs, beaten

2 tablespoons caraway seeds

2 tablespoons kosher salt

2 tablespoons olive oil

½ onion, finely chopped

3 large garlic cloves, minced

1 tablespoon tomato paste

½ cup dry red wine

2 fresh thyme sprigs or 1 teaspoon dried

2 pounds roast beef, thinly sliced

1 jar (5 ounces) prepared horseradish, about ½ cup

BEFORE YOU GO: The night before, heat oven to 375°F. Split rolls in half and put tops on a baking sheet. Brush tops with beaten egg and scatter on caraway and salt. Bake until seasonings adhere, about 5 minutes. Remove and let cool. Put rolls in large zipper-lock bags, seal, and stash in your carry-all bag.

Heat oil in medium saucepan over medium heat. When it's hot, add onion and cook until soft, about 5 minutes. Add garlic and cook 2 minutes. Stir in tomato paste, wine, and thyme. Increase heat to medium-high and simmer until liquid reduces by about half, 10 to 15 minutes. Remove from heat, cover, and let sit overnight.

Bring everything to the tailgate.

WHEN YOU GET THERE: Reheat tomato sauce over medium-low heat until hot, 5 to 10 minutes. For each sandwich, dip slices of roast beef in sauce until warm. Put several slices of dripping beef on bottom of roll, then add a heaping tablespoon of horseradish. Dip cut side of top of roll in sauce, then plunk onto the sandwich.

NEIGHBORLY TIP This sandwich is traditionally made with freshly roasted beef and the roast's pan juices. If you have a leftover roast, replace the prepared sauce in the recipe with the roast's pan juices. Otherwise, use thin slices of your favorite deli roast beef and the prepared sauce above.

The Vikings' Most Valuable Catcher

When you're featured in your favorite team's publications and commercials, odds are pretty good that you're a superfan. But when you pop up in not one, but two video games for your stadium antics, you *know* you're something special.

Syd Davy never bragged about his remarkable role in Minnesota Vikings home games. He just caught wide receiver Randy Moss in his arms whenever Moss scored a touchdown near Davy's seat. Davy caught Moss ten times since they started the tradition in 1998.

Davy is hard to miss in the crowd. Atop his head sits a horned Viking helmet with bright yellow braids of rope hair that dangle down his chest. His face is painted purple, and he wears purple camouflage pants and a massive belt buckle emblazoned with "VWO," for Viking World Order. Add a pair of arms that measure nineteen-plus inches at the biceps, complete with Vikings-theme tattoos, and you get a picture of this formidable fan.

The forty-six-year-old train engineer and his wife, who live in Winnipeg, Manitoba, make the thousand-mile round trip to Vikings home games at least ten times a season. "When I walk down the stairs to my seats at the start of the game," says Davy, "I get a standing ovation from fans, and people want to high-five me."

With appearances in *Sports Illustrated* and *Maxim* magazines, and his digitized likeness appearing in the video games *NFL Fever* and *Madden NFL 2005*, Davy's legacy as a fan for the ages is secure.

Philly Cheesesteak

My buddy Jeff Lockwood lives near Philadelphia about forty-five minutes south of me. We both have kids and run our own businesses, so we're pretty busy. But we try to meet up whenever we can to ride singlespeed mountain bikes or snowboard. Jeff's a cheesesteak connoisseur, if there is such a thing. He likes Jim's cheesesteaks on South Street, where they make the steaks with choice top round beef. But he admits, "No drunken trip to south Philly is complete without a dueling cheesesteak competition," which means "eating a Geno's steak, then crossing the street to down a Pat's. Always a regret in the morning!" Pat's, Geno's, and Jim's all make their cheesesteaks a little differently. And you can order the steaks with whatever toppings you like (see Tips). Here's a classic with onions and peppers. Jeff doesn't go for the peppers (sometimes not even the onions), but this is how I think the steaks taste best. I like to use sliced rib-eye beef because the meat oozes out a bit more grease and that's what makes the sandwich taste so good. **MAKES 6 SANDWICHES**

½ cup olive oil

2 small green bell peppers, seeded and thinly sliced

2 onions, chopped

2 pounds rib-eye or top round steak or roast, chipped (see Tips)

1½ teaspoons salt

¾ teaspoon ground black pepper

12 ounces (about 12 slices) provolone or American cheese or Cheez Whiz (see Tips)

6 submarine sandwich rolls, each 8 to 10 inches long and split but still in one piece

WHEN YOU GET THERE: For each sandwich, heat 1 heaping tablespoon oil in large skillet or griddle over medium heat. (Cook sandwiches in batches unless you have a huge-ass skillet or griddle.) Add peppers and onions and cook until soft, 5 to 8 minutes. If peppers take too long to cook, cover and "sweat" them into submission. Add meat and scatter on ¼ teaspoon of salt and ⅛ teaspoon of pepper. Chop meat repeatedly with stiff spatula during cooking. Cook until nicely browned all over, about 5 minutes, flipping and chopping. Gather the frying mess into a mound and lay two slices of cheese over it. When cheese starts to melt, put roll over mound for 15 seconds to warm up and soak up some juices. Put spatula under meat mound, your hand on top of roll, and flip meat into roll. Use spatula to tuck meat and veggies into roll. Lean forward as you eat the sandwich (the Philly lean) to avoid dripping grease all over yourself.

NEIGHBORLY TIPS Ask your butcher to shave or "chip" the beef as thinly as possible. If you're working with a thick steak or roast, stick the meat in the freezer for 20 to 30 minutes to firm it up. Then slice it as thinly as possible, no more than $\frac{1}{16}$ inch thick. Use a sharp knife or the slicing disk on a food processor. Bring the meat back to room temperature before cooking.

Purists skip the onions and peppers, while others add everything but the kitchen sink. A cheesesteak with onions is known as "cheese with" in Philadelphia. You choose your flavors. Some possibilities include sautéed mushrooms, pizza sauce, or Basic Tomato-Basil Sauce (page 117), ketchup, hot sauce, mustard, pickles, and pickled hot peppers.

Cheese is a matter of choice. Most Philadelphians swear by Cheez Whiz, while others (like myself) prefer sliced provolone or American. If you're using Whiz, just squirt about 2 tablespoons onto the roll, then lay the roll over the mound of frying meat as directed in the recipe.

Chicken Jambalaya

Like gumbo, this spicy Louisiana specialty is open to interpretation. The basic dish is similar to rice pilaf but with added vegetables and various types of pork, poultry, and/or seafood. I include sausage and shrimp here, since most people can get them. To switch things up, try ham, tasso, crab, crawfish, or whatever's best in your area. You'll see plenty of variations on this theme at Tigers Stadium during an LSU game.

MAKES 8 TO 10 SERVINGS

¼ cup peanut oil or vegetable oil

¾ teaspoon salt

½ teaspoon ground black pepper

1 pound boneless, skinless chicken thighs

1 pound andouille or other spicy smoked sausage, cut into slices or small cubes

1 large onion, chopped

3 large celery ribs, finely chopped

2 bell peppers (green and/or red), seeded and finely chopped

2 cups long-grain rice

2 large garlic cloves, minced

1 teaspoon dried thyme

1 teaspoon paprika

½ to 1 teaspoon cayenne

1 bay leaf

4 cups chicken broth

1 can (16 ounces) chopped tomatoes, with juice

2 tablespoons Worcestershire sauce

1 pound large shrimp, peeled and deveined

2 scallions (green and white parts), chopped

BEFORE YOU GO: The night before, heat 2 tablespoons of the oil in large saucepan or deep, wide skillet over medium heat. Scatter ¼ teaspoon of the salt and ¼ teaspoon of the pepper over chicken. When oil is hot, add chicken and cook just until lightly browned all over, 5 to 10 minutes, turning chicken once or twice. Remove to cutting board. When cool, cut into bite-size pieces.

Add 1 tablespoon of remaining oil to pot. When hot, add sausage and cook until browned all over, 5 to 10 minutes, turning a few times. Remove to cutting board with chicken.

Add onion, celery, and bell peppers to pan. Cook until all vegetables are tender, about 10 minutes, stirring a few times and scraping up brown bits from bottom of pan.

Spread veggies to sides of pan and pour remaining 1 tablespoon oil into center. When it's hot, stir in rice and garlic until well coated with oil and cook 1 to 2 minutes. Stir in thyme, paprika, cayenne, bay leaf, remaining ½ teaspoon salt, and remaining ¼ teaspoon pepper, mixing everything thoroughly. Stir in 3 cups of the broth, the tomatoes, and Worcestershire. Bring to boil over high heat. Stir in reserved chicken and sausage. Reduce heat to medium-low, cover, and simmer gently until rice is still a bit firm to the bite and a thin layer of liquid remains in the bottom of pan, 15 to 20 minutes. Cover, remove from heat, and let cool to room temperature. Chill in refrigerator or cooler overnight. Bring remaining 1 cup broth with you.

WHEN YOU GET THERE: Stir in shrimp and remaining 1 cup broth. Bring mixture to simmer over medium-high heat. Reduce heat to medium-low, cover, and simmer until shrimp are bright pink and firm and rice is tender, 10 to 12 minutes, stirring frequently. Remove bay leaf and serve sprinkled with scallions. Keep warm over very low heat.

NEIGHBORLY TIP If you can't find andouille sausage, use smoked hot sausage, chorizo (spicy Spanish or Mexican sausage), or kielbasa.

Butternut Squash Soup

Pull out this soup when you want to impress the guests. It's creamy, elegant, and re-fined, with soothing tastes of curry and coconut milk. **MAKES 4 MODEST SERVINGS**

1 tablespoon canola oil

1 tablespoon butter

½ onion, chopped

1 carrot, chopped

2 garlic cloves, minced

1½ teaspoons minced fresh ginger

1½ teaspoons Madras curry powder

1 medium butternut squash, peeled, seeded, and chopped

1½ to 2 cups vegetable or chicken broth

1 cup fresh or canned unsweetened coconut milk

¼ teaspoon salt

BEFORE YOU GO: Heat oil and butter in large saucepan over medium heat until hot. Add onion, carrot, garlic, ginger, and curry powder. Cook until carrots are soft, 5 to 8 minutes. Stir in squash and 1½ cups of broth and bring to a boil over high heat. Reduce heat to medium-low, cover, and simmer until squash is tender, about 15 minutes. Stir in coconut milk and salt and puree until smooth (or a lit-tle chunky, if you like) with a stick blender. Or puree in an upright blender or food processor, in batches if necessary. Heat through in pan, then taste and add more of any seasoning you think is lacking. Remove from heat and let cool to room temperature. Transfer to an airtight container and refrigerate until cold. Or trans-fer to a preheated thermos and keep warm until serving.

WHEN YOU GET THERE: For hot soup, transfer soup to a soup pot and reheat over medium heat (perfect for chilly weather). Or ladle the soup into bowls and serve cold or warm.

NEIGHBORLY TIPS To easily peel butternut squash, prick the skin several times with a fork. Microwave on high power until the skin softens, about 2 minutes. Peel from top to bottom with a vegetable peeler or paring knife. To make things even easier, look for peeled squash in your supermarket.

Canned unsweetened coconut milk is available in the international section of most grocery stores.

To gussy up the presentation, scatter minced red bell pepper and cilantro over the center of the soup. Garnish the soup before serving or set the garnishes in bowls for guests to use to decorate their own servings.

Party on Wheels
DIVIDED THEY FALL; UNITED THEY TAILGATE

K eith Moodie held season tickets to Giants games, but his girlfriend Elizabeth was a die-hard Eagles fan. How could such a doomed relationship work? Here's how: they took a panel truck, added some airbrushing, and drove off into a happy marriage.

The Bear, Delaware, couple first started tailgating out of their PT Cruiser but quickly outgrew that and graduated to a pickup truck. When that became too snug for their good times, they bought an old white panel truck for $500. After $2,500 of renovations, which included a couch, carpeting, two televisions, and a beautiful paint job, they dubbed her the Bluebird. Half the truck is painted blue with a Giants theme and the message Go Big Blue. The other half is painted green with a Fly Eagles Fly dedication.

Their wedding was held before a Giants/Eagles game, of course. The cake featured two helmets clashing, with goalposts rising above the little plastic bride and groom. Elizabeth wore her wedding dress into the stadium and Keith wore a custom-made Giants vest. ESPN filmed them for a commercial. The Eagles won the game, much to Keith's dismay, so now they have to see Elizabeth's team whenever both play on the same day.

Keith, a part-time event planner who's trying to become a professional tailgater, has this bit of advice for guys whose wives aren't so supportive of their game-day habits: "Try to get her involved. If she doesn't want to tailgate, then treat her to a nice dinner on Saturday night before you get into the doghouse on Sunday."

Seafood Chowder

My good friends Brian and Jen Fiske live in Maine, where seafood stewed with onions, potatoes, and milk or cream is known as "chowdah." Farther south, in the Carolinas and Georgia, a similar soup (minus the potatoes) is made with female crabs and their roe. Here's a blend of these two East Coast recipes, using both crab and shrimp in a creamy stew of onions, potatoes, and half-and-half, with a little bacon for extra flavor. This recipe is easy enough to make at the tailgate, but I make it the night before to get a jump on things. Try it at Gillette Stadium for a New England Patriots game. **MAKES 4 TO 6 SERVINGS**

3 slices thick-cut bacon, chopped

½ onion, chopped

1 garlic clove, minced

2 fresh thyme sprigs

1 bay leaf

4 cups (1 quart) half-and-half

2 large Yukon Gold or other yellow-fleshed potatoes, peeled and cut into bite-size pieces

1 tablespoon Worcestershire sauce

1 tablespoon dry sherry or white wine

1 teaspoon salt

½ teaspoon ground black pepper

1 pound medium shrimp, peeled and deveined

8 ounces lump crabmeat, picked over to remove cartilage

2 scallions (green and white parts), chopped

BEFORE YOU GO: Put bacon in medium soup pot over medium-low heat and cook until crisp, 10 to 15 minutes. Add onion and garlic and cook until onion is tender, 5 to 8 minutes. Add thyme, bay leaf, half-and-half, and potatoes. Bring to a boil over high heat, then reduce heat to medium-low, cover, and simmer until potatoes are tender, about 15 minutes. Stir in Worcestershire, sherry or wine, salt, and pepper and simmer, uncovered, 10 minutes. Remove from heat and let cool to room temperature. Cover and chill in refrigerator or cooler overnight.

WHEN YOU GET THERE: Reheat chowder over medium heat. When it's hot, add shrimp and cook until bright pink and firm, about 10 minutes. Stir in crab and heat just until crab is warmed through, about 5 minutes. Taste and add more of any seasoning you think is lacking. Remove bay leaf and thyme sprigs. Top with scallions.

NEIGHBORLY TIPS You can replace the shrimp and crab with other seafood such as chopped clams, lobster, or white-fleshed fish.

For thicker chowder, cook the potatoes until very tender, then mash some with the back of a spoon and stir into liquid to thicken.

Party on Wheels
THE RAVENS' SWAT TEAM

If you see a big black police vehicle barreling down the highway near Baltimore on an NFL game day, you might find it heading toward a good time rather than a crime in progress. In an earlier life, this panel truck was a Snyder's of Hanover snack-delivery vehicle. Then the Ravens' fan club—the SWAT Team (Stop Working and Tailgate)—had it painted black with official Ravens logos and police-type shields on the doors. The shields show a swooping raven clutching a line marker in one claw and a sausage impaled on a barbecue fork in the other. The SWAT Team also installed swiveling lights and a siren on the roof.

The vehicle is now known as the Emergency Response Tailgate Unit (ERTU) and is staffed by some of Charm City's most highly trained tactical tailgaters.

Championship Chili

I developed this chili for my buddy Dale Mack years ago. He's been serving it at games ever since. Dale sometimes uses ground turkey instead of beef. I've even made the chili with crumbled veggie burgers for vegetarians. You choose your favorite protein. Either way, this New Mexico–style beef-and-bean chili rocks. Dale claims it's even helped the Cowboys to beat the Eagles. **MAKES 10 TO 12 SERVINGS**

1 pound ground chuck

2 medium onions, chopped

4 garlic cloves, chopped

2 medium carrots, chopped

2 red bell peppers, seeded and chopped

2 to 4 jalapeño chiles, seeded and chopped

2 cans (28 ounces each) chopped tomatoes (with juice)

4 cans (15 ounces each) black beans, rinsed and drained

2 cups beer

Juice of 2 fresh limes

2 tablespoons chili powder

1 tablespoon ground cumin

1 tablespoon dried oregano

1 teaspoon salt

½ teaspoon ground black pepper

½ cup chopped fresh cilantro

Hot pepper sauce

BEFORE YOU GO: The night before, cook beef in large soup pot over medium heat until no longer pink, about 5 minutes. Remove beef to bowl and drain off all but 1 tablespoon fat from pan. Add onions, garlic, carrots, bell peppers, and jalapeño chiles to fat in pan. Cook until vegetables are soft, about 8 minutes. Add chopped tomatoes (with juice) and cook 5 minutes. Add beans, beer, lime juice, about ½ cup water, chili powder, cumin, oregano, salt, black pepper, and reserved beef.

Bring to boil over high heat. Reduce heat to medium-low and cook until nice and thick, about 45 minutes. Remove from heat and let cool. Cover and chill in refrigerator or cooler.

WHEN YOU GET THERE: Reheat chili over medium-low heat. When reheated, if chili is too thick, add more beer and/or water. If it's too thin, raise heat to medium and cook until thickened. Keep warm over low heat.

Scatter on cilantro and hot pepper sauce to taste.

NEIGHBORLY TIPS For Vegetarian Black Bean Chili, replace the beef with frozen vegetarian burger crumbles and cook the crumbles in 1 tablespoon olive oil in the soup pot. Proceed with the recipe as directed.

You could make this chili the morning of the tailgate if you have time. To transport it warm, wrap it in two layers of foil, then in a thick towel. It should stay warm for 2 hours. Reheat at the game.

For a Chili Cheese Dog, grill up your favorite frank, stuff it in a bun, and top with some of this chili and some shredded Cheddar cheese.

Tame the Flames

Heat seekers sometimes overdo it when eating spicy food. If you've bitten off more flame than you can chew, cool down with a dairy product. Milk, yogurt, ice cream . . . they all do the trick. That's because dairy fat intervenes between the pain receptors in your mouth and the chile's hot compound, known as capsaicin.

Texas Red

Popularized in San Antonio, chili is known throughout Texas as simply "a bowl of red." That means red meat, red chile peppers, and maybe a few other ingredients. Definitely no beans. Leave that to the cooks in New Mexico. And if you're a real purist, skip the tomatoes, too. Chile and beef should be what you taste. That said, the whole idea is to make it your own with your favorite add-ins. You like beer? Pour it in. You want it real hot? Load up on fiery chiles like cayenne or pequín. Want onions and cheese on top? By all means. Here's my favorite way to start up a bowl of basic Texas red. The recipe owes a tip of the hat to Texans Joe Cooper and Frank Tolbert, two early champions of the dish who both paved the way for generations of Texas chilis to come. I prefer to use whole ancho chile peppers, but here I opt for dried ancho powder to save time. Look for ancho powder in glass bottles in the spice aisle of your grocery store, or in a Mexican grocery store. You'll need a few bottles. You'll pay a few bucks for that convenience. But it's worth it. Option two is to visit a Mexican grocer and buy about ten whole ancho chile peppers, which are dirt cheap, then toast the pods in a dry skillet, remove the stems and seeds, and grind the pods to a powder in a spice grinder. Your choice: spend a little more time or a little more money. **MAKES 8 TO 10 SERVINGS**

4 pounds lean beef chuck, cut into bite-size pieces

¾ cup ancho chile powder

¼ cup hot paprika

1½ cups beef stock

1 bottle or can (12 ounces) beer

5 garlic cloves, minced

2 tablespoons ground cumin

2 tablespoons dried oregano

1 teaspoon cayenne, or more to taste

2 teaspoons salt

2 teaspoons sugar

½ teaspoon ground black pepper

2 tablespoons masa harina or cornmeal

BEFORE YOU GO: The night before, heat a soup pot over medium-high heat until hot. Drop in beef and cook in dry skillet, stirring and scraping bottom constantly until meat is grayed over and starts to release some juices, 3 to 5 minutes. Stir in ancho powder and paprika and cook until fragrant and starting to thicken, 1 to 2 minutes. Add stock and enough beer to just cover beef. Bring to a boil, then reduce heat to medium-low, cover, and simmer 45 minutes. Stir now and then, adding beer as necessary to keep meat just covered.

Add garlic, cumin, oregano, cayenne, salt, sugar, and black pepper. Cover and simmer, stirring now and then, until meat is as tender as a baby's bottom, about 30 minutes. Sip the beer while the chili cooks, adding beer to the pot as necessary to keep the meat covered. Crack open new beers as necessary.

Mix masa harina or cornmeal with a couple tablespoons of beer. Stir into pot until chili thickens up a bit, then cover and simmer another 15 minutes, stirring occasionally, and adding beer as necessary. Taste the chili often, adding a little more of any seasoning you think is lacking.

Remove from heat and cool to room temperature. Or cool slightly, then chill covered pot in refrigerator on an oven mitt or pot holder until cold. Transfer covered pot to cooler.

WHEN YOU GET THERE: Reheat chili over medium-low heat until hot, about 20 minutes, adding more or less beer to thin or thicken. Thin or thick is your choice: I like my chili with a gravy the consistency of thick tomato sauce. Keep on low heat all day to keep improving the flavor.

NEIGHBORLY TIPS To save chopping time, look for stew beef that's already cut or ask your butcher to cube the chuck for you.

If you're using store-bought beef broth, look for the kind sold in aseptic packaging rather than in cans. Aseptically packaged broths undergo a flash heating and cooling process that helps the broth retain more flavor.

Masa harina is Mexican cornmeal, a coarse flour made from lime-soaked corn kernels that are cooked, ground, and then dried.

For a smoky taste, replace the cayenne pepper with chipotle powder.

Venison Stew

The first venison I tasted was at my friend Len's house in North Caldwell, New Jersey. Len and his father would go to Pennsylvania to hunt deer. One day when we were teenagers, Len took me out to his garage to show me the catch. Len's father was a terrific Italian cook, so I knew he would be serving up that venison in all sorts of great ways. I missed most of the dishes because Len and I lived thirty miles apart. But I do remember the stew they served. It was thick with meat juices and red wine; the only vegetables were carrots and onions; and the meat tasted a lot like beef, but with less fat and a cleaner flavor. Now I live in Pennsylvania and neighbors always talk about their venison: the chops they pan-fried, the tenderloin they roasted, or the stew they simmered. Here's a good, basic venison stew reminiscent of the first one I ever ate. Make it ahead and take it to a fall tailgate with crusty bread to soak up the juices. **MAKES 6 TO 8 SERVINGS**

4 ounces (about 4 slices) thick-cut sliced bacon, finely chopped

2 pounds venison chuck roast, trimmed of fat and
cut into 1-inch chunks

1 teaspoon dried thyme

1 teaspoon salt

1 teaspoon ground black pepper

1 onion, coarsely chopped

2 garlic cloves, minced

⅓ cup all-purpose flour

1½ cups beef stock

1 to 1½ cups dry red wine

1 tablespoon Worcestershire sauce

2 bay leaves

1 teaspoon paprika

½ teaspoon dried savory or sage

1 bottle or can (12 ounces) beer, preferably dark

2 pounds new or red-skinned potatoes (4 to 5 medium), peeled and cut into
½-inch chunks

1 pound carrots (about 4 large), peeled and cut into ½-inch chunks

1 to 2 tablespoons tomato paste

BEFORE YOU GO: The night before, cook bacon in large stew pot or Dutch oven over medium-low heat until crisp, about 15 minutes. Remove bacon to a bowl or cutting board with slotted spoon. Sprinkle venison with thyme, ½ teaspoon of the salt, and ½ teaspoon of the pepper. Increase heat to medium-high and add venison to pot in batches to avoid crowding. Cook meat until well browned all over, 5 to 8 minutes, removing chunks as they're done. Add onion and garlic and cook until soft, about 5 minutes. Stir in flour and cook 2 minutes. Add browned meat and bacon along with stock, 1 cup of wine, Worcestershire, bay leaves, paprika, savory or sage, remaining ½ teaspoon salt, remaining ½ teaspoon pepper, and just enough beer, if necessary, to halfway cover meat. Scrape bottom of pan to loosen all the browned bits. Bring to a boil, then reduce heat to low, cover, and simmer gently until meat is tender, 1½ to 2 hours. Add more wine or beer as necessary to keep meat just halfway covered with liquid. Stir in potatoes and carrots. Bring to a boil over high heat, then reduce heat to medium-low, cover, and simmer until vegetables are tender, about 1 hour. Taste and add more of any seasoning you think is lacking. Remove from heat and let cool to room temperature. Cover and chill in refrigerator or cooler overnight or up to 3 days.

WHEN YOU GET THERE: Reheat stew over medium-low heat until heated through, about 20 minutes. Add wine or beer as necessary to thin stew. If liquid is too runny, stir in just enough tomato paste to thicken. Remove bay leaves and serve in bowls.

NEIGHBORLY TIPS I like to use chuck for stewing but any cut from the shoulder would do.

If you're using the meat of a wild-caught (rather than farmed) animal, marinate the cubed meat to help tenderize and flavor it. Two nights before the tailgate, use half of the wine, beer, garlic, onion, Worcestershire, paprika, savory or sage, salt, and pepper to make the marinade in a large freezer-weight zipper-lock bag. Add meat and chill in refrigerator or cooler overnight. The night before the tailgate, remove meat from marinade, pat dry, and continue with recipe. Add the marinade along with the other half of the liquids and seasonings when called for in the recipe.

If using store-bought beef broth, look for the kind sold in aseptic packaging rather than in cans. Aseptically packaged broths undergo a flash heating and cooling process that helps the broth retain more flavor.

Chicken Gumbo

Gumbo isn't just a stew. It's Southern history in a bowl. Gumbo is so intrinsic to Louisiana culture that the team mascot of the New Orleans Saints is named Gumbo the Saint Bernard. This now classic dish slowly developed as African slaves and others living in Louisiana, including Spanish and Native Americans, added their own favorite ingredients to the fish stew favored by French settlers. The word gumbo actually derives from the African word for okra, a green pod vegetable that many consider essential. But ingredients vary from okra to lima beans to chicken to turkey to ham to sausage to shrimp to crawfish to oysters. The point is: toss in what you like. As with many gumbos, this one has seen several incarnations in my kitchen over the years. Serve it in bowls with cooked rice. **MAKES 8 TO 10 SERVINGS**

⅔ cup peanut oil or vegetable oil

¾ teaspoon salt

¾ teaspoon ground black pepper

12 ounces boneless, skinless chicken thighs

12 ounces fresh or frozen okra, trimmed and sliced ¼ inch thick, about 2 cups

1 onion, chopped

1 green bell pepper, seeded and chopped

2 celery ribs, chopped

3 garlic cloves, minced

½ cup all-purpose flour

3 to 4 cups chicken broth

2 cans (16 ounces each) stewed tomatoes, with juice

12 ounces andouille sausage, cut into slices or small cubes

2 bay leaves

¼ to ½ teaspoon cayenne

1 pound medium shrimp, peeled and deveined

1 pound lump crabmeat, optional

2 teaspoons filé powder, optional

4 scallions (green and white parts), chopped, optional

3 tablespoons chopped fresh parsley, optional

BEFORE YOU GO: The night before, heat 2 tablespoons of oil in large soup pot over medium heat. Scatter ¼ teaspoon of the salt and ¼ teaspoon of the pepper over chicken. When oil is hot, add chicken and cook just until no longer pink in center, 5 to 10 minutes, turning chicken once or twice. Remove to cutting board. When cool, shred with a fork or cut with the grain into thin strips.

Add another 2 teaspoons oil to pot. When hot, add okra and cook until tender, 5 minutes. Add onion, pepper, celery, and garlic. Cook until all vegetables are tender, about 10 more minutes, stirring a few times. Transfer vegetables to bowl.

Add remaining ½ cup oil to pot. Gradually whisk in flour. Reduce heat a little and cook, whisking frequently, until mixture (the roux) starts to thicken and turns medium brown, about 8 minutes. Watch carefully so the roux doesn't burn. It should be a nutty dark brown color. If it burns, clean the pot and start over again with fresh oil and flour. Gradually whisk in 3 cups of broth. Stir in reserved chicken and vegetables, tomatoes, sausage, bay leaves, cayenne, remaining ½ teaspoon salt, and remaining ½ teaspoon pepper. Bring to boil over high heat. Reduce heat to medium-low and simmer gently, uncovered, for 45 minutes. Let cool to room temperature, then cover and refrigerate in pot.

WHEN YOU GET THERE: Bring pot to boil over medium-high heat. Reduce heat to medium and fish out bay leaves. Add remaining stock if you like a thinner stew. Stir in shrimp and crabmeat, if using, and cook until the shrimp are bright pink, about 5 minutes. Taste and add more salt and pepper as necessary. Keep over low heat and allow guests to stir about ¼ teaspoon filé, if using, into each serving. Garnish with scallions and parsley, if using.

NEIGHBORLY TIPS If you can't find andouille sausage, use another spicy smoked sausage, chorizo, or kielbasa.

Filé powder is the ground leaves of the sassafras tree. Look for it in the spice aisle of your grocery store or check the ingredient sources on page 184. You could also leave it out. The gumbo will be plenty thick and tasty without it.

It's a good idea to keep some hot sauce on hand for those folks who like their gumbo to bite back.

Cajun Deep-Fried Turkey

Deep-fried turkey originated in Cajun country and has become popular all over the South. You'll see turkeys in fry pots everywhere from Kansas City's Arrowhead Stadium to the Georgia Dome to the Louisiana Superdome. The technique has spread like wildfire among tailgaters. There are a few tricks to make sure you don't burn the turkey or yourself. But otherwise, the beauty of deep-fried turkey lies in its simplicity: fry a big bird and feed a big crowd. **MAKES 8 TO 10 SERVINGS**

CAJUN INJECTION MARINADE

⅓ cup water

2 tablespoons honey

1 tablespoon paprika

1 tablespoon salt

2 teaspoons ground black pepper

1 to 2 teaspoons cayenne

1 teaspoon garlic powder

1 teaspoon onion powder

½ teaspoon dried thyme, crushed

½ teaspoon dried oregano, crushed

½ teaspoon dry mustard

TURKEY AND OIL

One 10- to 12-pound turkey, preferably fresh

4 to 5 gallons peanut oil or canola oil

BEFORE YOU GO: The night before, put everything but the turkey and oil in a small saucepan over medium-low heat. Heat until warmed through and honey melts, stirring several times, 3 to 4 minutes. Let cool slightly, then suck marinade up into a seasoning injector or kitchen syringe (in batches if necessary). Add water to the injection marinade by the teaspoon, if necessary, to thin out enough for your injector.

Remove turkey giblets and neck. Rinse turkey inside and out with cold water and pat dry. Put turkey in roasting pan and inject mixture all over turkey (in legs, thighs, wings, and breast) until all of mixture is used. Cover with plastic wrap and refrigerate overnight.

WHEN YOU GET THERE: Remove turkey from cooler 20 minutes before frying. Put an outdoor gas burner in an open area away from cars, tents, etc. Put large deep pot (7 to 10 gallons) onto burner and pour oil into pot. Check that oil will not over-flow when turkey is lowered into pot. Heat oil to 375° to 390°F, which will take about 30 minutes. Turn off burner before adding turkey. Put turkey, neck down, into fry basket or rack. Wearing oven mitts or silicone gloves (and protective eye-wear if you're really jittery), grab basket or rack handle and slowly lower turkey into hot oil. Or use a firmly trussed turkey and put a broomstick through loop of string. With one person on each end of broomstick, slowly lower turkey into hot oil. Oil will sputter briefly and temperature will lower. Turn burner back on and adjust heat to maintain oil temperature of 350° to 360°F (if temperature drops to 340°, oil will seep into turkey and make it greasy). Fry until an instant-read thermometer registers 180°F when inserted into a breast or until a leg tears off easily when tested, 30 to 40 minutes (3 to 4 minutes per pound). Carefully remove turkey from oil and let drain. Wearing grill mitts or silicone gloves, trans-fer to a serving platter and let rest 20 minutes before carving. Cool the oil com-pletely before storing or disposing.

NEIGHBORLY TIPS Pick up a seasoning injector at a cookware store or from The Barbecue Store in the gear section on page 182. These are great for putting fla-vor right into meats rather than just on the surface. Other tools you'll need here: 7 to 10 gallon deep-frying pot with insert basket (or a trussed turkey and a broomstick); outdoor gas burner and propane; frying or candy thermometer; and instant-read thermometer. Check the gear section to buy any of these items.

To re-use the oil (which is expensive in large amounts), let it cool to about 100°F, then pour it through a coffee filter into a clean plastic bucket with a tight-fitting lid. Seal and store in the refrigerator or a cool, dark spot such as a basement or cellar.

Dispose of large amounts of spent oil by taking it to your local landfill. Or call a local restaurant. Most restaurants have used grease bins. Ask if you can add your used oil to their grease bin.

Fry Safely

When deep-frying a turkey, always use your head. Keep in mind that beer should probably be left out of the recipe.

Here's how to fry a turkey without getting burned.

- Keep an all-purpose fire extinguisher nearby, and never use water to extinguish a grease fire.

- Only use your turkey fryer outdoors a safe distance from any buildings or other materials that will burn.

- Never leave the fryer unattended. Since most units don't have a thermostat, the oil in the fryer will continue to grow hotter until it catches fire if you don't intervene.

- Keep children and pets away from the hot fryer. Even after you turn it off, the oil remains hot for several hours.

- Avoid overfilling the fryer with oil. Leave enough room at the top for the oil level to rise when the turkey is lowered into the pot. If you're unsure, fill the fryer with water and dunk in the turkey as a test. Remove the turkey, then mark where the water line is so you don't put too much oil in the fryer and end up with an overflow of oil everywhere.

- Use insulated pot holders or oven mitts when touching pot or lid handles. Heatproof silicone gloves are even better.

- Only fry a thawed turkey. If you marinate the bird, reduce oil spattering by completely drying the surface of the turkey before lowering it into the hot oil.

FROM THE
Thermos

Cold Drinks	Hot Drinks
Bloody Mariachi	Hot Applejack Cider
One-Two Punch	Spiked Wine
Sangría	Mocha Madness
Long Island Iced Tea	Hot Buttered Rum

Bloody Mariachi

Here's a Bloody Mary for those who like a loud wake-up call. It's got a Mexican kick with tequila, lime, and smoky chipotle chiles in place of the traditional vodka, lemon, and Tabasco. **MAKES 6 SERVINGS**

3 cups (24 ounces) tomato juice

1 cup plus 2 tablespoons (9 ounces) good tequila

2 tablespoons (1 ounce) fresh lime juice

1 tablespoon (½ ounce) Worcestershire sauce

1 to 2 teaspoons adobo liquid from canned chipotle chiles

¼ teaspoon ground black pepper

¼ teaspoon celery salt

6 celery sticks, optional

BEFORE YOU GO: The morning of the tailgate, pre-chill a 2-quart thermos by filling it with ice and/or cold water and refrigerating for 5 minutes. If you don't have a thermos, use a pitcher or other container with a tight-fitting lid. Dump out ice water and mix in everything but celery salt and celery sticks, if using. Stir, taste, and add more of any ingredient you think is lacking. Screw on lid and take along.

WHEN YOU GET THERE: For each drink, pour about ¾ cup into an ice-filled glass or cup. Add a pinch of celery salt on top and swizzle with celery sticks, if using.

NEIGHBORLY TIP Canned chipotle chiles or "chipotles en adobo" are a common canned good in Mexican groceries. You can also find them in the international aisle of many supermarkets. The adobo is a smoking-hot canning liquid made from ground chiles, tomatoes, vinegar, and herbs. A typical 7-ounce can of chipotles in adobo has about 3 tablespoons adobo liquid. Use the chipotles or their canning liquid anywhere you want some serious heat and smoke. If you can't find them, substitute about 1 teaspoon chipotle powder, which grocery stores typically carry in glass bottles in the spice aisle.

One-Two Punch

Punch is open to your imagination. And whenever I start dreaming, I think tropical. That means mango, orange, pineapple, and lime. And a one-two punch of rum. Yum! **MAKES 8 TO 10 SERVINGS**

1 can (12 ounces) mango nectar

1 can (12 ounces) unsweetened pineapple juice

1½ cups (12 ounces) orange juice

½ cup (4 ounces) fresh lime juice

½ cup (4 ounces) dark or spiced rum

½ cup (4 ounces) light rum

Dash of Angostura bitters, optional

1 cup (8 ounces) sparkling water or club soda, optional

BEFORE YOU GO: The morning of the tailgate, pre-chill a 2-quart thermos by filling it with ice and/or cold water and refrigerating for 5 minutes. If you don't have a thermos, use a pitcher or other container with a tight-fitting lid. Dump out ice water and mix in everything but sparkling water, if using. Stir, taste, and add more of any ingredient you think is lacking. Screw on lid and take along.

WHEN YOU GET THERE: For each drink, pour about ¾ cup into an ice-filled glass or cup. Add about 2 tablespoons sparkling water to fizz things up if you like; otherwise, leave the drink straight over ice. Or pour the punch and sparkling water, if using, into a punch bowl, then let guests ladle servings into ice-filled cups.

NEIGHBORLY TIPS Mango nectar by Goya is sold in cans in the international aisle or juice aisle of many grocery stores. They sell cans of pineapple juice, too, but you could use any unsweetened pineapple juice.

Most supermarkets also carry Angostura bitters near the club soda and bottled drink mixes.

For a morning tailgate, turn this into modified mimosas. Replace the sparkling water with champagne.

To decorate the punch bowl, float in a few sprigs of mint and/or some edible flowers like calendula and nasturtiums.

Sangría

I first made sangría for a backyard fiesta in the late 1980s. When it got dark and the sangría was gone, the party stragglers sucked the wine-soaked oranges right out of their skins. I joined them and was forever hooked. Sangría is a great party drink because it's a good alternative to beer and goes with lots of different grilled foods. Save this cold drink for a warm-weather game like the Orange Bowl or Cotton Bowl. If it's chilly out, try the hot Spiked Wine (page 148). **MAKES 10 SERVINGS**

4 oranges

1 lime

1 lemon

1 large bottle (1.5 liters) dry red wine

2 tablespoons (1 ounce) brandy

2 tablespoons (1 ounce) orange liqueur, such as Cointreau, Grand Marnier, or Triple Sec

⅔ cup sugar

2 cinnamon sticks

10 whole cloves

5 whole allspice berries

2 cups (16 ounces) sparkling water or club soda, chilled

BEFORE YOU GO: Up to 2 days before, use a vegetable peeler to remove peel of one orange in a continuous strip without removing any bitter white membrane. Put peel in a 2- to 3-quart pitcher or container with a tight-fitting lid. Squeeze in the juice of the peeled orange, two more oranges, half the lime, and half the lemon. Cut remaining orange into 8 wedges. Thinly slice remaining lime and lemon, adding all fruit to container along with all but ½ cup of the wine.

In small microwaveable bowl, combine reserved ½ cup wine, brandy, orange liqueur, and sugar. Microwave just until warm, about 30 seconds. Stir until sugar dissolves, then add cinnamon sticks. Wrap cloves and allspice in coffee filter or cheesecloth and seal with clean twist-tie. Drop spice bundle into warm liquor mixture. Swirl a few seconds, then pour all into wine mixture. Chill in refrigerator or cooler at least 2 hours or up to 2 days.

WHEN YOU GET THERE: Remove orange peel and spice bundle. For each drink, pour about ¾ cup into an ice-filled glass or cup and add about ¼ cup sparkling water. Or pour the sangría and sparkling water into a punch bowl, then let guests ladle servings into ice-filled cups.

Long Island Iced Tea

This has got to be the ultimate party drink. It tastes like Coke, gets everyone totally looped, and the proportions are easy to remember. For each serving, you dump a tablespoon of five different liquors into a glass, a tablespoon of fresh lemon juice, and ½ can of Coke. I multiplied the recipe here to serve eight happy partygoers. Here's a mnemonic device to help you remember all the ingredients: Vinnie T! Let's Get Really Tanked! With Coke! (Vodka, Triple sec, Lemon juice, Gin, Rum, Tequila, Coke.) **MAKES 8 SERVINGS**

½ cup (4 ounces) vodka

½ cup (4 ounces) Triple Sec

½ cup (4 ounces) fresh lemon juice, from **2 to 3 lemons**

½ cup (4 ounces) gin

½ cup (4 ounces) rum

½ cup (4 ounces) tequila

1½ quarts Coca-Cola

8 lemon wedges, optional

BEFORE YOU GO: The morning of the tailgate, pre-chill a 1-quart thermos by filling it with ice and/or cold water and refrigerating for 5 minutes. If you don't have a thermos, use a pitcher or other container with a tight-fitting lid. Dump out ice water and mix in booze and lemon juice. Stir, taste, and add more of any ingredient you think is lacking. Screw on lid and take along.

WHEN YOU GET THERE: For each drink, pour about ⅓ cup of booze mixture into an ice-filled glass or cup. Pour in about ¾ cup chilled Coca-Cola (half a 12-ounce can). Garnish with lemon wedge if desired.

Hot Applejack Cider

Beer is king at tailgates but hot cider helps to warm up the crew on those bitter cold days. Pour in some applejack and everyone gets happy. Add some apple schnapps and now you've got a party! Applejack is an American apple brandy similar to France's Calvados. Look for straight applejack instead of blended versions. Straight gives you a better hit of apple flavor. Same goes for the schnapps. Beware of "imitation liqueurs." For the best taste, pick up some pure apple schnapps like Berentzen's Apfel Korn. **MAKES 8 TO 10 MUGFULS**

2 quarts apple cider

¼ cup packed brown sugar

Peel of 1 orange, removed in a continuous strip

6 cinnamon sticks (plus 8 to 10 more for garnish, optional)

12 whole cloves

12 whole allspice berries

1 cup (8 ounces) straight applejack or Calvados

½ cup (4 ounces) pure apple schnapps

BEFORE YOU GO: The night before, put cider, brown sugar, orange peel, and cinnamon in medium pot over medium heat. Wrap cloves and allspice in a coffee filter or cheesecloth and seal with a clean twist-tie. Drop spice bundle into cider and heat over medium heat until cider just starts to simmer, 15 to 20 minutes. Reduce heat to low and heat for 1 hour. Turn off heat, cover, and let sit overnight.

To serve from a thermos, reheat cider the next morning over medium heat until hot, about 10 minutes. Preheat a 2-quart thermos by filling it with hot water and letting sit 5 minutes. Pour out hot water and put solids from pot into thermos. Then pour in cider (strain the cider if the brown scum bothers you). Screw on lid and take along.

To serve from a pot, see Tips below.

WHEN YOU GET THERE: Remove and discard solids and pour cider from thermos into mugs, adding 1 ounce (2 tablespoons) applejack or Calvados and ½ ounce (1 tablespoon) apple schnapps to each mug. Garnish each mug with a cinnamon stick if you like.

NEIGHBORLY TIPS To serve from the pot, bring pot of cider mixture (with spices) to the tailgate. If your pot doesn't have a tight-fitting lid, transfer cider mixture to a 2-quart pitcher or container with a tight-fitting lid. Reheat in pot over medium heat until hot, about 15 minutes. Ladle into mugs, adding 1 ounce (2 tablespoons) applejack or Calvados and ½ ounce (1 tablespoon) apple schnapps to each mug.

When you peel the orange, use a gentle hand to avoid removing any of the bitter white membrane from the orange, which could make the cider taste bitter.

A slice of fresh apple in each mug gives you extra points. Or to get real fancy, cut the orange into wedges instead of removing the strip of peel. Add the wedges to the cider and brew. When serving, stick fresh whole cloves in each wedge and put a clove-studded orange wedge in each cup.

If you have time, you could make this entire recipe at the game, leaving the cider to steep over low heat for a few hours instead of chilling and then reheating it.

Add 3 to 4 pieces of whole star anise to the spice bundle for an anise flavor.

Spiked Wine

When cold weather rolls around, I always heat up a pot or two of spiced wine. Sure, I like a good dark beer in the winter, but mulled wine is more festive. This hot drink is perfect for tailgates in December and January when you're in the holiday mood. It's similar to a traditional Swedish celebration wine called glögg, but without the raisins and almonds. If some Swedish tailgaters happen to drop by, impress them by serving mugfuls of the wine with a few raisins and almonds dropped into each mug.

MAKES 8 TO 10 MUGFULS

1 tangerine

12 whole cloves

6 whole allspice berries

6 slices fresh ginger, unpeeled

6 cinnamon sticks

1 large bottle (1.5 liters) dry red wine

¾ cup (6 ounces) brandy or vodka

½ cup sugar

BEFORE YOU GO: The night before, cut tangerine in half crosswise and stick cloves into peel of both halves. Put in a 2-quart thermos, pitcher, or other container with a tight-fitting lid. Wrap allspice and ginger in coffee filter or cheesecloth and seal with clean twist-tie. Add spice bundle to container along with cinnamon and wine. Put on lid and chill in refrigerator or cooler overnight.

To serve from a thermos, empty contents into medium pot the next morning. Pour in brandy and sugar, then heat over medium heat until almost simmering, stirring to dissolve sugar. Reduce heat to medium-low and heat 20 minutes. Preheat a 2-quart thermos by filling it with hot water and letting sit 5 minutes. Pour out hot water and pour in hot wine. Screw on lid and take along.

To serve from a pot, see Tips below.

WHEN YOU GET THERE: Remove solids and pour wine from thermos into mugs.

NEIGHBORLY TIPS To serve from a pot, pour the container contents into a medium pot when you get to the tailgate. Stir in the brandy and sugar, then heat over medium heat until almost simmering, stirring to dissolve the sugar. Reduce the heat to medium-low and heat 20 minutes. Ladle into mugs. In this case, you could make this drink in the same pot you will serve it from, as long as the pot has a tight lid and you're sure the wine won't spill all over your car in transit.

Look for a dry, fruity red wine. Don't spend a fortune, but don't buy a wine you wouldn't drink straight. If you've got some ruby port on hand, add about ½ cup to the mix for a fuller flavor.

For more spice flavor, add 6 to 8 crushed cardamom pods to the spice bundle.

You Don't Know Jack About Tailgating

A mouthwatering rib recipe or high-tech grill might make you think you're a world-class party host. But when the folks at Jack Daniel's crown you their annual tailgating champ, you have extra reason to strut.

Each football season, JD's Great American Tailgate Search sends party buses around the country to award trophies, T-shirts, and jerseys to the most outstanding tailgating crews in each city. They look for "creativity, team spirit, and creative food and drink preparation." Take note, though, if the judges think you're objectionable you're given the boot. That presumably means everyone needs to keep their pants on, and probably their shirts, too.

Celebrity judges include folks like the Master Distiller at the company's Lynchburg, Tennessee, distillery, and the great-great-grandniece of Jack Daniel himself.

If your group takes first prize in your city *and* your NFL team makes it to the championships, you win a trip on a bus tour that culminates in a cook-off at the Super Bowl. Head on over to www.jackdaniels.com for more details.

Mocha Madness

Before the days of cheap cocoa powder and dried milk, people made hot chocolate by melting chocolate bars in hot milk. Add some coffee and you double your caffeinated pleasure. Add some booze and you triple the pleasure! Some call this drink a mocha, like the ones you get at trendy coffee shops. I call it a good way to warm up on a cold day. **MAKES 8 TO 10 MUGFULS**

2 cups (16 ounces) strong brewed coffee

4 ounces bittersweet chocolate, chips or bar

½ cup packed brown sugar

Pinch of salt

1 quart milk

1 teaspoon cinnamon

¼ cup (2 ounces) bourbon

¼ cup (2 ounces) brandy

¼ cup (2 ounces) Kahlúa

2 teaspoons vanilla extract

Whipped cream, optional

BEFORE YOU GO: The morning of the tailgate, brew coffee, then put chocolate, ¼ cup water, the brown sugar, and salt in medium pot. Heat over medium-low heat, stirring until chocolate melts, about 15 minutes. Gradually stir in milk, coffee, and cinnamon. Heat until hot, about 10 minutes. Remove from heat and stir in bourbon, brandy, Kahlúa, and vanilla.

To serve from a thermos, preheat a 2-quart thermos by filling it with hot water and letting sit 5 minutes. Pour out hot water and pour in mocha madness. Screw on lid and take along.

To serve from a pot, see Tips below.

WHEN YOU GET THERE: Pour into mugs and top with whipped cream, if using.

NEIGHBORLY TIPS To serve from a pot, cover the pot you're using if you're sure it won't spill in transit. Otherwise, let cool slightly and transfer to a 2-quart container with a tight-fitting lid. At the tailgate, return the mocha madness to the pot and reheat over medium-low heat until hot, about 15 minutes. Top with whipped cream, if using.

For a richer drink, use 2 cups milk and 2 cups light cream or half-and-half.

If you want to get really drunk, double the bourbon, brandy, and Kahlúa. It still tastes like hot chocolate, but with a solid dose of booze.

Canned whipped cream works in a pinch, but fresh is so much better. To make it, stash ½ pint heavy cream, a metal whisk or beaters for an electric mixer, and a medium metal or glass bowl in the coldest part of your cooler. When you're ready to serve the madness, pour the cream into the bowl and whisk or beat at medium speed until the cream forms soft peaks when the whisk or beaters are lifted. Whisk in 2 teaspoons vanilla extract and 2 tablespoons sugar, confectioners' sugar, or corn syrup (these last two help to stabilize the cream better than granulated sugar). Dollop onto each mug of mocha madness and savor the insanity.

Hot Buttered Rum

Years ago, during a cold November party, my wife and I served hot buttered rum from our stovetop. We set everything out—mugs, rum, butter, and a kettle of water—so guests could make the drinks themselves. The rum was gone so fast we decided to make a triple batch the next time around. We've tried several versions over the years, including some made with ice cream, but we like this one best for tailgates. If you don't use all of the spiced butter, just chill it or freeze it until next time. **MAKES 12 MUGFULS**

12 tablespoons (1½ sticks) butter, softened

2 tablespoons brown sugar

1½ teaspoons apple pie spice

1 teaspoon vanilla extract

3 cups (24 ounces) dark or spiced rum

¾ cup (6 ounces) pure maple syrup

2 to 3 quarts boiling water

12 cinnamon sticks, optional

BEFORE YOU GO: Mix softened butter, brown sugar, apple pie spice, and vanilla until blended in 1-cup container with tight-fitting lid. Seal and chill in refrigerator or cooler up to 3 weeks.

WHEN YOU GET THERE: For each serving, pour about ¼ cup (2 ounces) rum and 1 tablespoon (½ ounce) maple syrup into a mug. Fill with boiling water and float 1 tablespoon butter mixture on top. Stir with a cinnamon stick, if using, or spoon to mix in maple syrup and begin melting butter.

NEIGHBORLY TIPS Boil water at the game. Or preheat a 2-quart thermos with hot water, then re-fill it with fresh hot water and bring it along. If you have enough hot water, preheat the mugs with hot water before adding the other ingredients.

For a more complex flavor, use a mixture of rums: half dark or spiced rum and half light rum. A squeeze of fresh lemon adds another layer of flavor.

If you don't have apple pie spice, mix together ½ teaspoon each ground cinnamon, nutmeg, and allspice, plus ¼ teaspoon ground cloves.

IN THE
Bag

Breakfast

Big John's Baked Eggs

French Toast Casserole

Snacks and Cookies

Chipotle Pecans

Bourbon Bombs

Champion Chip Cookies

Picnic Main Dishes

Tomato-Olive Goat Cheese Tart

Buttermilk Fried Chicken

Corn Bread and Desserts

Jalapeño Beer Corn Bread

Apple Streusel Galette

Heavy-Duty Chocolate Bread Pudding

Big John's Baked Eggs

Big John and Linda Gavin run the Texans Tailgaters Club. John likes to eat these eggs before Houston Texans games, followed by fajitas after. Take John's advice and serve the eggs with your favorite hot sauce. John's top choice: Tapatío hot sauce. Buttered toast or tortilla chips go well here, too. **MAKES 6 SERVINGS**

1 pound loose breakfast sausage, hot or mild

1 small onion, finely chopped

2 garlic cloves, minced

1 can (4 ounces) mild chopped green chiles, drained

1 package (8 ounces) shredded Cheddar-Jack cheese

1 dozen large eggs

½ cup milk

½ teaspoon salt

½ teaspoon ground black pepper

BEFORE YOU GO: The morning of the tailgate, heat oven to 475°F. Mix sausage, onion, and garlic in 2-quart baking dish; cook in oven until sausage is browned and onion is soft, 10 to 12 minutes, stirring a few times and breaking up sausage. Remove pan from oven and reduce heat to 325°F.

Scatter chiles and half of cheese over sausage. Mix eggs, milk, salt, and pepper in large bowl. Pour evenly into pan and scatter on remaining cheese. Bake until browned on top and no longer jiggly in middle, 45 to 55 minutes. Remove from oven and let cool slightly. Cover with a double layer of foil and wrap in cloth towels (big, thick bath towels are best). When wrapped, this casserole will stay warm for 3 to 4 hours. Carry it in a bag or just in the back of your vehicle.

WHEN YOU GET THERE: Slice into squares and serve warm.

NEIGHBORLY TIPS To make an even heartier dish, mix 1 cup cooked hash browns into the sausage before pouring on the eggs.

John also suggests crumbling 2 slices cooked crispy bacon over the eggs before baking.

To add more savory flavor, mix 1 teaspoon dried thyme or poultry seasoning in with the eggs.

Gators Spawn a Drink Industry

Thanks to the University of Florida, athletes from the pros down to the weekend warriors can refill their tanks on hot days with a drink that helps them perform better.

In 1965, a Florida Gators coach and a university kidney specialist tried to figure out why the football players were losing so much weight during practices and games. They realized that players were sweating out buckets of salt, potassium, and other electrolytes in the southern heat.

The academics concocted a batch of water, salt, sugar, and lemon juice to remedy the situation. Players who drank it tended to perform better on the field, and Gatorade was born. The Stokely–Van Camp Company started marketing the beverage nationally in 1967. Since 1973, when a legal battle over royalties was settled, Gatorade has fattened the university's coffers by more than $90 million. In 2001, PepsiCo, Inc., bought the Gatorade brand, but the University of Florida still gets royalties on sales.

French Toast Casserole

During the summer, I'm a surf rat. I love going to the Atlantic coast and riding the waves. The past few years, we've been getting our kicks in Avalon, New Jersey, a sleepy beach town south of Atlantic City. We sometimes stay at the Sealark Bed & Breakfast, run by Pat Ellis and John Oldham. Pat always has great breakfasts. She was kind enough to share this recipe with me and it's since become a hit at tailgates. To keep it warm, wrap the casserole in foil and then in thick bath towels. The bread doesn't stay quite as crisp as it is fresh from the oven, but the flavor is still great. The early arrivals at your tailgate will be glad you brought this to the game. By the way, if you have stale bread, use it. It softens as it soaks up the eggs overnight.

MAKES 10 SERVINGS

1 small loaf (8 ounces) stale French bread, cut into 1-inch cubes (8 to 10 cups)

8 large eggs

3 cups milk

5 tablespoons sugar

2 teaspoons vanilla extract

3/4 teaspoon salt

2 tablespoons butter, cut into small pieces

3/4 teaspoon cinnamon

Maple syrup

BEFORE YOU GO: The night before, grease a 13 × 9-inch baking dish with butter, oil, or cooking spray. Put bread cubes in dish. Beat eggs, milk, 4 tablespoons of the sugar, the vanilla, and salt in medium bowl. Pour over bread. Cover and refrigerate overnight.

The next morning, remove from fridge 20 minutes before baking. Heat oven to 350°F. Dot casserole with butter and combine remaining 1 tablespoon sugar with cinnamon; scatter over top. Bake until a knife inserted near center comes out clean, about 45 minutes. Let cool slightly, then cover with a double layer of foil and wrap in cloth towels (big, thick bath towels are best). When wrapped, this casserole will stay warm for 3 to 4 hours. Carry it in a bag or just in the back of your vehicle.

WHEN YOU GET THERE: Unwrap, slice, and serve with maple syrup.

NEIGHBORLY TIP To make Apple French Toast Casserole, lay 2 cored, peeled, and sliced apples over the bottom of the greased dish. Scatter an extra 1 tablespoon sugar mixed with ¼ teaspoon cinnamon and ½ teaspoon flour over the apples. Top with bread cubes and continue with recipe.

Cornholing in Cincinnati

If you're going to tailgate in Cincinnati, you'd better brush up on your cornhole first. Now, get your mind out of the gutter: we're talking about the game "cornhole," the game, not any vulgar slang term. The game is similar to horseshoes, only players hurl six-inch corn-filled bags instead of equestrian footwear and aim for two slanted boxes with a six-inch hole in each as targets instead of stakes.

It's also called "Baggo," and you'll find tailgaters playing the game all over America's parking lots. Two teams of two people try to throw their bags into the opposing target thirty feet away. Players get three points for a bag that goes into the hole, and one point for a bag that's either resting on the playing surface, clinging to the hole, or hanging off the edge of the playing surface but not touching the ground.

In Cincinnati, cornholing is so popular that the city has hosted a Cornhole Classic tournament, and the parking lots around the Paul Brown Stadium are filled with the sounds of Bengals fans cornholing before games.

Who says the Midwest isn't as exciting as the coasts?

Chipotle Pecans

Munch on these addictive nuts on the way to the game. If you plan to eat some at the game, make a double batch. The nuts don't stick around very long. I like the smoky flavor of ground chipotle chiles here; it gets my tongue ready for the taste of grilled foods to come. But if you can't find chipotle chile powder, cayenne will give you the heat without the smoke. **MAKES 2½ CUPS**

1 egg white

⅓ cup sugar

1½ teaspoons chipotle powder or cayenne

1½ teaspoons salt

½ teaspoon pure chile powder (such as ancho)

¼ teaspoon unsweetened cocoa powder

¼ teaspoon cinnamon

2½ cups pecan halves

BEFORE YOU GO: Preheat oven to 325°F. In medium bowl, using electric mixer on medium speed, beat egg white until very foamy and no clear liquid remains. Stir in everything but pecans until blended. Stir in pecans until evenly coated. Spread in single layer on an ungreased baking sheet.

Bake until fragrant and toasted, 20 to 25 minutes. Remove from oven and let cool 5 minutes. Loosen and break up nuts with stiff spatula (nuts may be gooey but will crisp as they cool). Cool completely in pan on rack. Store cooled nuts in an airtight container up to 1 week.

WHEN YOU GET THERE: Pass them around (if there's any left).

NEIGHBORLY TIP Most grocery stores carry pure chile powder and chipotle powder in the spice aisle. Look in the "gourmet" section of spices in glass bottles.

Bourbon Bombs

These little candies are like rum balls made with bourbon instead. Mix up these Kentucky sweets a couple or three days before you go. They taste better after mellowing a bit. **MAKES ABOUT 50 BOMBS**

½ cup bourbon

3 tablespoons light corn syrup

2 cups confectioners' sugar

3 tablespoons unsweetened cocoa powder, preferably Dutch process

½ teaspoon cinnamon

¼ teaspoon salt

¾ cup pecan halves or pieces

1 package (12 ounces) vanilla wafer cookies

BEFORE YOU GO: In large bowl, mix bourbon and corn syrup. Whisk in 1¼ cups of the confectioners' sugar, the cocoa powder, cinnamon, and salt until smooth.

Toast pecans in small, dry skillet over medium heat until fragrant, shaking pan now and then, 3 to 5 minutes. Finely chop pecans in food processor or by hand. Stir into bourbon mixture.

Crush cookies into crumbs in food processor or in a big zipper-lock bag using a rolling pin or heavy pan. Stir crumbs into bourbon mixture (it will be stiff). Let sit 5 minutes.

Put remaining ¾ cup confectioners' sugar in a shallow bowl. Roll bombs into 1-inch balls between your palms (or roll into football shapes if you want to get fancy), then roll in confectioners' sugar. Store at room temperature in an airtight container between layers of wax paper for up to 2 weeks.

NEIGHBORLY TIPS Dutch-process cocoa powder has an alkali added during processing that helps to neutralize the natural acidity of cocoa beans and make the flavor less bitter. This type makes a good choice in recipes where raw cocoa is mixed with only a few ingredients. Most grocery stores sell it. Even Hershey's makes it.

A whisk is the best tool for the job when mixing in lumpy dry ingredients like confectioners' sugar and cocoa powder. A fork would do in a pinch. Or you could sift these ingredients into the bowl for absolute uniformity.

Champion Chip Cookies

Sometimes I just want a serious hit of chocolate. That's when I break out these over-size double-chocolate-chip-pecan cookies. What you taste is chocolate, chocolate, and more chocolate. When cooled, these chocolate chippers are soft and chewy all over. Just the way I like 'em. If you want, you can halve the recipe. But believe me, thirty-six cookies don't last long at a tailgate. A note of thanks to my baking heroes Nick Malgieri, Carole Walter, Elinor Klivans, and Maida Heatter. I've been making their cookies for years and this cookie was inspired by bits of wisdom from all of them. **MAKES ABOUT THIRTY-SIX 3½-INCH COOKIES**

1¾ cups flour

¾ cup unsweetened cocoa powder, preferably Dutch process

1½ teaspoons baking soda

¾ teaspoon salt

½ pound (2 sticks) unsalted butter, softened (see Tips)

¾ cup packed light brown sugar

¾ cup granulated sugar

2 tablespoons light corn syrup

2 large eggs

2 teaspoons vanilla extract

2 cups bittersweet or semisweet chocolate chips

1½ cups pecan halves, coarsely chopped

BEFORE YOU GO: The night before, put oven racks in upper and lower thirds of oven. Heat oven to 350°F and line two large baking sheets with foil. Whisk flour, cocoa powder, baking soda, and salt in medium bowl until relatively free of cocoa lumps.

Put butter, brown sugar, granulated sugar, and corn syrup in large bowl and beat with electric mixer on medium speed until blended and creamy, about 1 minute. Beat in eggs and vanilla on low speed. Stir in flour mixture with a spoon. Stir in chips and nuts and chill dough 10 minutes.

Drop by 2-inch balls (about the size of an average ball hitch) about 2 inches apart on prepared sheets. Bake just until cookie centers look dull instead of shiny, 10 to 12 minutes. Cookies will feel soft to the touch but resist the temptation to bake further. Cool 5 minutes in pan. Slide foil off baking sheet to transfer entire batch of cookies to cooling rack. Loosen from foil when cookies are firm enough to hold their shape. Cool completely on cooling rack.

Using two cookie sheets, you'll need to do two separate bakings. Put fresh foil on the baking sheets after previous batches are removed. Put cookie dough in fridge between batches to keep dough from softening too much. When all cookies are completely cooled on rack, transfer to crushproof, airtight container.

WHEN YOU GET THERE: Munch away, if there's any left from the car ride to the tailgate.

NEIGHBORLY TIPS For more flavor, toast the pecans on one of the baking sheets in the oven as it preheats. Shake the pan once or twice and remove the nuts when they smell fragrant and toasty, after 5 to 8 minutes.

To reheat the cookies at the game, bring along a cookie sheet. Line the sheet with foil and put the cookies on the foil. Put the sheet on the grill over medium-low heat (perfect for when the coals die down), then put the lid down and heat just until soft and warm, 3 to 5 minutes.

To quickly soften butter, cut into several pieces in microwaveable bowl and microwave in 10-second increments until just soft enough to be dented with a finger but not lose its shape.

If you have trouble with your cookies spreading too much, chill the dough for 30 minutes before baking and check your oven temperature with an oven thermometer. Ovens can be off by as much as 100°F from what's listed on the dial. It also helps to put the filled cookie sheet onto an empty cookie sheet, which creates a layer of insulation between the sheets and promotes more even heating.

Tomato-Olive Goat Cheese Tart

This egg-and-vegetable pie falls into the category of "lighter" tailgate fare. Picnic food, really. Generally, I prefer to make tart crusts from scratch, but the flat, refrigerated pastry sheets come in handy when time is short. These sheets of pie dough are sold two in a package, usually in the refrigerated dough section of the grocery store (near the "poppin' fresh" biscuits, cinnamon rolls, and such). You'll need only one pastry sheet for this recipe. Use the other to make Apple Streusel Galette (page 168) or freeze for another use. The best thing about this recipe, aside from the rustic French flavors, is that you just assemble and bake it, then bring it to the tailgate. No hardcore cooking. Perfect for an early fall tailgate or brunch before a noon game.

MAKES 6 SERVINGS

Half a 15-ounce package refrigerated pie crust sheets (not in a tin)

2 tablespoons Dijon mustard

½ cup shredded Gruyère cheese

2 ripe tomatoes, sliced ¼ inch thick

½ cup pitted niçoise or kalamata olives

½ teaspoon salt

¼ teaspoon ground black pepper

2 tablespoons torn fresh tarragon

3 large eggs

8 ounces soft goat cheese, at room temperature

2 to 4 tablespoons milk

BEFORE YOU GO: The night before, preheat oven to 400°F. Put a 9-inch tart pan with removable bottom on a baking sheet. Unroll pie crust into the pan. Gently lift and push dough into sides and bottom of pan. Trim any overhang by running a rolling pin over pan. Prick bottom and sides of dough a few times with a fork. Bake until lightly browned, about 15 minutes. Cool on baking sheet. Cover with a kitchen towel.

The next morning, preheat oven to 375°F. Brush or spread mustard over pie shell. Sprinkle with ¼ cup of the Gruyère. Arrange half of tomato slices over Gruyère. Scatter half of olives around tomatoes and sprinkle with half of salt, pepper, and tarragon. Make another layer with remaining tomatoes, olives, salt, pepper, and tarragon. Whisk eggs and goat cheese in medium bowl. Whisk in just enough milk to thin the mixture to a pourable consistency similar to thick pancake batter. Pour egg mixture evenly over tomatoes, spreading to fill in gaps and evenly cover the ingredients. Sprinkle with remaining ¼ cup Gruyère. Bake until set and lightly browned on top, 25 to 30 minutes.

Remove from oven and let cool slightly. Cover with a double layer of foil and wrap in cloth towels (big, thick bath towels are best). When wrapped, tart will stay warm for 2 to 3 hours. Carry it in a bag or just in the back of your vehicle.

WHEN YOU GET THERE: Keep wrapped until serving time, then unwrap and cut into wedges. Unwrapped tart will stay warm about 30 minutes and can be served at room temperature for another hour.

Buttermilk Fried Chicken

Good fried chicken takes a watchful eye to keep the fry oil at the right temperature. If the oil is too hot, the crust burns before the meat is done cooking. If it's too low, the crust and meat soak up too much fat and taste greasy. Otherwise, it's pretty simple to make. A buttermilk marinade here helps to tenderize and flavor the chicken. And a little baking powder in the flour helps the crust to puff up so it tastes crunchier. Bring this to a Clemson Tigers game and swap fried chicken recipes with your tailgating neighbors. **MAKES 4 SERVINGS**

2 cups buttermilk

1 teaspoon sugar

5 teaspoons salt

2 teaspoons ground black pepper

³/₄ teaspoon cayenne

3½ to 4 pounds bone-in chicken breasts, thighs, and drumsticks

2 cups flour

1 tablespoon baking powder

About 3 cups vegetable shortening, lard, olive oil, or peanut oil

BEFORE YOU GO: Mix buttermilk, sugar, 2 teaspoons of the salt, ½ teaspoon of the black pepper, and ¼ teaspoon of the cayenne in 2-gallon freezer-weight zipper-lock bag. Drop in chicken, seal, and chill overnight in refrigerator or cooler.

Early the next morning, mix together flour, baking powder, and remaining 3 teaspoons salt, 1½ teaspoons black pepper, and ½ teaspoon cayenne in large paper or plastic bag. Using tongs, transfer a few chicken pieces to bag and shake to coat. Remove to a rack and let rest 15 to 20 minutes. Repeat with remaining chicken pieces.

Melt shortening over medium-high heat in a deep, heavy frying pan such as cast iron. The shortening should be about ½ inch deep and hot enough to make a small piece of chicken sizzle loudly when dipped in, about 350°F on a candy or frying thermometer. Using tongs, put chicken pieces, skin side down, in pan without crowding (work in batches if necessary). Reduce heat to medium, cover, and cook until bottom is darkly browned, 10 to 12 minutes. Adjust heat to keep fat between 250° and 300°F. Turn and cook, uncovered, until other side is darkly browned and meat registers about 170°F in breasts and 180°F in thighs and drumsticks. Transfer to rack to cool slightly. Transport on rack loosely covered with wax paper or in a paper bag to keep crisp and warm. Avoid wrapping in foil, which will steam the crust and make it soggy.

WHEN YOU GET THERE: Chicken will be safe to eat at room temperature for 3 to 4 hours after cooking. To hold longer, transfer cooled chicken to a doubled paper bag, close bag, and chill in refrigerator or cooler. Serve cold or at room temperature.

NEIGHBORLY TIPS For Spicy Fried Chicken: Add 2 tablespoons chili powder to the flour mixture.

Cast-iron pans make the best fried chicken because they help to keep the fat at an evenly hot temperature.

You could fry the chicken the day before the tailgate and chill it overnight in the fridge. The crust will lose some crispness, but you won't have to do any cooking the morning of the tailgate.

For less fat, oven-fry the marinated chicken instead. Replace the flour coating with 2 cups seasoned dried bread crumbs; or use a mixture of 3 cups crushed breadsticks or Wheat Thins crackers, ½ teaspoon black pepper, ½ teaspoon salt, and ¼ teaspoon cayenne. Coat chicken with crumbs, then spray coated chicken with cooking spray. Heat a baking sheet in 425°F oven until sheet is hot, then add chicken, skin side down, and bake until meat is cooked to temperatures given in recipe above, turning once, 30 to 40 minutes.

For even less fat, remove the chicken skin (where most of the fat is contained) before marinating. Dip the skinless marinated chicken pieces in a mixture of 2 beaten egg whites, 2 teaspoons cornstarch, and the juice of half a lemon to help the coating adhere. Put the coating in a shallow bowl and roll the chicken in the egg white mixture, then in the coating, and proceed with oven-frying as described above.

Jalapeño Beer Corn Bread

My wife, Christine, has been a vegetarian for more than a decade. Vegetarians eat a lot of beans, especially in soups, stews, and chili. Nothing beats chili and corn bread at a late-fall tailgate, except maybe chili and jalapeño corn bread (and beer!). Over the years, we've made pans and pans of different kinds of corn bread: sweet, plain, white, yellow, with buttermilk, with jalapeños, with kernel corn, as pancakes, and, before Christine was vegetarian, with bacon drippings and butter instead of vegetable oil. But we always come back to our basic Southern corn bread that was inspired by Sara Wade Robbins's recipe in Sundays at Moosewood Restaurant by the Moosewood Collective. I've tinkered with Sara's recipe over the years, but no significant improvements have been made to the original. Except the addition of jalapeño and beer. **MAKES 6 TO 8 SERVINGS**

2 eggs

½ cup buttermilk

½ cup beer (ale or lager)

¼ cup vegetable oil

¼ cup packed light brown sugar

1 teaspoon salt

4 teaspoons baking powder

1 cup yellow cornmeal (stone ground is best)

1 cup all-purpose flour

1 to 2 jalapeño chiles, seeded and chopped

BEFORE YOU GO: The morning of the tailgate, heat oven to 400°F. Grease a 10-inch round cast-iron skillet or other 1½-quart baking dish.

Whisk eggs, buttermilk, beer, oil, brown sugar, and salt in large bowl until blended. Scatter baking powder over top and whisk until blended. Mix in cornmeal, flour, and jalapeños, gently stirring until batter is almost free of lumps. Pour into skillet or dish and bake until a knife inserted in center comes out clean, 15 to 20 minutes. Cool slightly on a rack. Cover with a double layer of foil and wrap in cloth towels (big, thick bath towels are best). When wrapped, corn bread will stay warm for 3 to 4 hours. Carry it in a bag or just in the back of your vehicle.

WHEN YOU GET THERE: Cut into wedges and serve.

NEIGHBORLY TIPS You can replace the fresh jalapeños with pickled or canned.

For richer corn bread, replace 2 tablespoons of the vegetable oil with 2 tablespoons butter or bacon drippings.

For a crisp bottom crust, heat the pan in the oven while you mix the ingredients. Melt an extra tablespoon butter in the pan. When it's hot, pour in the batter and bake.

For Jalapeño Beer Cheese Corn Bread, stir in ½ cup shredded Cheddar or Jack cheese along with the jalapeños.

If you like your corn bread while it's still hot, cook the corn bread in an ovenproof skillet such as cast iron and reheat the bread in the skillet on your grill over medium-low heat with the lid down.

If you want to wimp out on the jalapeño and beer, just ditch the jalapeño and replace the beer with milk.

Apple Streusel Galette

A galette is simply an open-faced pie. It's a nice change of pace from a two-crust pie and real easy to put together, especially if you use store-bought pie dough. The best thing about this galette for tailgating is that it has a homemade feel, yet you don't have to carry home any dirty dishes. Just slide the galette onto a large picnic plate, then cut and serve it when you get there. **MAKES 6 SERVINGS**

3 to 4 medium tart apples, peeled, cored, and sliced (about 1½ pounds)

4 tablespoons granulated sugar

5 tablespoons flour

¾ teaspoon cinnamon

¼ teaspoon salt

3 tablespoons butter

¼ cup packed light brown sugar

¼ cup finely chopped walnuts

Half a 15-ounce package refrigerated pie crust sheets (not in a tin)

BEFORE YOU GO: Up to 1 day before, heat oven to 375°F. Mix apples, 3½ tablespoons of the granulated sugar, 1 tablespoon of the flour, ¼ teaspoon of the cinnamon, and ⅛ teaspoon of the salt in medium bowl.

Put 2 tablespoons of the butter in microwave-safe medium bowl. Microwave on high until just melted, about 30 seconds. Mix in brown sugar, nuts, and remaining 4 tablespoons flour, ½ teaspoon cinnamon, and ⅛ teaspoon salt.

Unroll pie crust on an ungreased flat cookie sheet or back of a rimmed baking sheet (using the flat side makes it easier to slide the galette onto a plate after it's cooked). Arrange apples in a mound over center of dough, leaving a 2-inch border of dough. Scatter brown sugar topping over apples. Working around the circle of apples, lift border of dough over edge of apples, folding dough every 3 to 4 inches to make a pleat so dough lies evenly. About 6 to 7 inches of streusel topping will still be visible in center after dough is folded around edges. Gently press dough onto filling with your hands.

Wipe out bowl used to make streusel topping. Add remaining 1 tablespoon butter and microwave on high until just melted, about 30 seconds. Brush melted butter over exposed edge of pie dough. Sprinkle dough with remaining 1½ teaspoons granulated sugar. Pour any remaining butter over streusel topping.

Bake until dough is lightly browned and apples are tender when tested with a knife, 30 to 40 minutes. Cool on a rack. Loosen with a spatula and slide onto a big picnic plate. Transport loosely covered to serve warm. Or cool completely, cover, and serve at room temperature. Will keep up to 1 day.

WHEN YOU GET THERE: Cut and serve.

NEIGHBORLY TIPS Granny Smith is the classic tart apple for pies, but try others like Macoun, Jonathan, or Gala. Taste a slice of apple as you work. If it tastes more sweet than tart, add 1 to 2 teaspoons lemon juice to the apple mixture.

Look for flat refrigerated sheets of pie crust in the refrigerated dough section of your grocery store near the refrigerated biscuits.

Serve with whipped cream or half-and-half poured around the edges.

Heavy-Duty Chocolate Bread Pudding

My uncle Bill shared this dessert with me during a big barbecue in 2004. It was gone before most people knew it was there. The five ingredients are croissants, chocolate, cream, egg yolks, and sugar. How can you go wrong? Add a scoop of ice cream and it's total nirvana. **MAKES ABOUT 12 GENEROUS SERVINGS**

Butter, for greasing

1½ pounds good-quality semisweet chocolate, such as Scharffen Berger, Valrhona, or El Ray

3 cups (1½ pints) heavy cream

8 egg yolks

½ cup sugar, plus some for dusting

6 to 8 croissants, sliced and cubed

BEFORE YOU GO: Use a butter wrapper to grease inside of a deep, round 4-quart baking dish (in a pinch use a rectangular 15 × 10-inch pan, but a deeper pan is better). Dust the inside with sugar, shaking to coat completely.

Preheat oven to 325°F. Put chocolate and cream in medium saucepan over medium-low heat. Cook, stirring now and then, until chocolate melts. Keep warm over low heat.

In large bowl, mix together egg yolks and sugar. Stir in about ½ cup of chocolate mixture to gradually bring egg yolks up in temperature. Stir in remaining chocolate mixture until blended. Stir in cubed croissants. Scrape into baking dish and bake until most of the shine disappears from the top (wet parts should be mostly cooked), about 45 minutes for a deep dish or 30 minutes for wider, shallow pan.

Remove from oven and let cool slightly. Cover with a double layer of foil and wrap in cloth towels (big, thick bath towels are best). When wrapped, pudding will stay warm for about 3 hours. Carry it in a bag or just in the back of your vehicle.

WHEN YOU GET THERE: Keep wrapped until serving time. Unwrap and serve with spoons and bowls. Unwrapped pudding will stay warm about 30 minutes and can be served at outside temperature for another hour.

NEIGHBORLY TIPS Pick up the croissants from your local bakery or coffee shop.

Look for good-quality chocolate in specialty markets or see the sources on page 184. If that fails, Ghirardelli brand from the grocery store will do.

To keep the bread pudding extra moist, sit the baking pan in a larger pan half full with hot tap water. The water should come about halfway up the baking pan and will help to gently cook the pudding and keep it moist.

If the pudding cools off by the time you get to the game, don't worry. It's great at room temperature, too.

Tailgating
MENUS

If you really want to enjoy your tailgate, keep the menu simple. Don't go overboard. It's a party after all and you should enjoy it, too. Do most of the prep at home. If gametime is early, plan on a simple casserole, some sandwiches, quick-grilled foods, or other easy pre-game dishes that don't require long prep or cooking time in the parking lot. Chances are you'll be hungry after the game, so that may be the best time to fire up your grill as the post-game traffic thins out. Of course, if you'll be watching the game on a TV set in the parking lot, you can eat, drink, and cook all day long.

Here are a few menus to try the next time you hit the pavement. Some are for football bowl games or big rivalry matches held every year. Others are for NASCAR events, other sporting events, or just some good combinations of dishes to try out. If you want to cook the competition, try Buffalo Burgers (page 80) when you're playing the Bills, or Miami Dolphin-fish Steaks (page 108) when you're up against the Dolphins. If you can't beat 'em, eat 'em! Of course, it's always appropriate to serve up foods with *your* team colors to rally the troops.

NFL

CHICAGO BEARS VS. GREEN BAY PACKERS

Brats in Beer (page 68) or Gridiron Grinder (page 49)

Venison Stew (page 134) or Championship Chili (page 130)

Barbecue Beans (page 116)

DALLAS COWBOYS VS. PHILLY EAGLES

Texas Red (page 132) or Philly Cheesesteak (page 122)

Jalapeño Beer Corn Bread (page 166) or Grilled Corn on the Cob (page 58)

Chocolate Whiskey Pudding (page 52) or Champion Chip Cookies (page 160)

OAKLAND RAIDERS VS. KANSAS CITY CHIEFS

Tequila Tri-Tip (page 86) or Chipotle-Bourbon Ribs (page 74)

Grilled Corn Salad with Honey-Lime Dressing (page 43) or Creamy Slaw (page 41)

Heavy-Duty Chocolate Bread Pudding (page 170) or

Chocolate Whiskey Pudding (page 52)

PITTSBURGH STEELERS VS. CLEVELAND BROWNS

Venison Stew (page 134) or Beer Butt Chicken (page 98)

Spicy Steak Fries (page 59) or Grilled Corn on the Cob (page 58)

Hot Applejack Cider (page 146)

NFC CHAMPIONSHIP GAME

Buffalo Burgers (page 80) or Meatball Hero (page 118)

Pesto Tortellini Salad (page 48) or Black Bean Two-Cheese Quesadillas (page 61)

Chocolate Whiskey Pudding (page 52) or Champion Chip Cookies (page 160)

AFC CHAMPIONSHIP GAME

Beer and Coffee Steaks (page 84) or Venison Stew (page 134)

Tapenade (page 34) with bagel chips or Jalapeño Beer Corn Bread (page 166)

Apple Streusel Galette (page 168) or Bourbon Bombs (page 159)

SUPER BOWL BLOWOUT

Cajun Deep-Fried Turkey (page 138) or Smoky Rubbed Ribs (page 72)

Buffalo Chicken Wings (page 90) or Championship Chili (page 130)

Spinach Artichoke Bread Bowl (page 36) or

Red, White, and Blue Potato Salad (page 44)

Simple Salsa (page 39) and chips

Champion Chip Cookies (page 160)

PRO BOWL CELEBRATION

Swordfish Steaks with Pineapple Relish (page 106)

Chipotle-Lime Shrimp with Grilled Salsa (page 100)

Chinese Noodle Salad (page 46)

Grilled Pound Cake and Bananas Foster (page 112)

NCAA

FLORIDA STATE VS. MIAMI
Smoky Rubbed Ribs (page 72) or Miami Dolphinfish Steaks (page 108)
Black-Eyed Pea Salsa (page 40) or
Grilled Corn Salad with Honey-Lime Dressing (page 43)
One-Two Punch (page 143)
Piña Colada Cake (page 54)

**GEORGIA VS. FLORIDA, "THE WORLD'S LARGEST
OUTDOOR COCKTAIL PARTY"**
Buttermilk Fried Chicken (page 164) or Rum-Cardamom Pork Chops (page 70)
Red, White, and Blue Potato Salad (page 44) or Creamy Slaw (page 41)
One-Two Punch (page 143)
Bourbon Bombs (page 159) or Piña Colada Cake (page 54)

OREGON VS. OREGON STATE, "THE CIVIL WAR"
Maple-Rosemary Planked Salmon (page 104) or Barbecued Chicken (page 94)
Cooked rice or Creamy Slaw (page 41)
Apple Streusel Galette (page 168) or Heavy-Duty Chocolate Bread Pudding (page 170)
Spiked Wine (page 148) or Hot Buttered Rum (page 152)

STANFORD VS. CAL, "THE BIG GAME"
Black Bean Two-Cheese Quesadillas (page 61) or
Tapenade (page 34) with sliced baguette
Tomato-Olive Goat Cheese Tart (page 162) or Chinese Noodle Salad (page 46)
Tequila Tri-Tip (page 86) or Swordfish Steaks with Pineapple Relish (page 106)
Heavy-Duty Chocolate Bread Pudding (page 170) or
Grilled Pound Cake and Bananas Foster (page 112)

TEXAS VS. OKLAHOMA, "THE RED RIVER SHOOTOUT"
Big John's Baked Eggs (page 154) or Grilled Stuffed French Toast (page 110)
Beer-Mopped Brisket with Texas Barbecue Sauce (page 88) or
Beer and Coffee Steaks (page 84)
Spicy Steak Fries (page 59)
Chipotle Pecans (page 158) or Champion Chip Cookies (page 160)

NCAA

AUBURN VS. ALABAMA

Buttermilk Fried Chicken (page 164) or Cajun Deep-Fried Turkey (page 138)

Jalapeño Beer Corn Bread (page 166)

Black-Eyed Pea Salsa (page 40)

Chipotle Pecans (page 158)

MICHIGAN VS. OHIO STATE

Brats in Beer (page 68) or Gridiron Grinder (page 49)

Barbecue Beans (page 116) or Pesto Tortellini Salad (page 48)

Champion Chip Cookies (page 160) or Buckeye Candy (page 50)

ARMY VS. NAVY

Spinach Artichoke Bread Bowl (page 36) or Beer Boiled Shrimp (page 102)

Gridiron Grinder (page 49) or Buffalo Burgers (page 80)

Champion Chip Cookies (page 160) or Bourbon Bombs (page 159)

SEC CHAMPIONSHIP GAME

Chipotle-Bourbon Ribs (page 74) or Cajun Deep-Fried Turkey (page 138)

Black-Eyed Pea Salsa (page 40) or Red, White, and Blue Potato Salad (page 44)

Chocolate Whiskey Pudding (page 52) or

Grilled Pound Cake and Bananas Foster (page 112)

BIG 12 CHAMPIONSHIP GAME

Beer-Mopped Brisket with Texas Barbecue Sauce (page 88) or

Championship Chili (page 130)

Red, White, and Blue Potato Salad (page 44) or Grilled Corn on the Cob (page 58)

Champion Chip Cookies (page 160) or Chocolate Whiskey Pudding (page 52)

WAC CHAMPIONSHIP GAME

Buffalo Fajitas (page 82) or Beer-Butt Chicken (page 98)

Grilled Corn Salad with Honey-Lime Dressing (page 43) or Creamy Slaw (page 41)

Apple Streusel Galette (page 168) or Heavy-Duty Chocolate Bread Pudding (page 170)

NCAA

ROSE BOWL

Tuscan White Bean Salad (page 42) or
Grilled Corn Salad with Honey-Lime Dressing (page 43)
Tomato-Olive Goat Cheese Tart (page 162)
Tequila Tri-Tip (page 86)
Heavy-Duty Chocolate Bread Pudding (page 170)

FIESTA BOWL

Black Bean Two-Cheese Quesadillas (page 61) or Barbecue Beans (page 116)
Texas Red (page 132) or Beer-Mopped Brisket with Texas Barbecue Sauce (page 88)
Jalapeño Beer Corn Bread (page 166)
Sangría (page 144)
Chocolate Whiskey Pudding (page 52)

SUGAR BOWL

Creamy Slaw (page 41) or Red, White, and Blue Potato Salad (page 44)
Chicken Gumbo (page 136) or Chicken Jambalaya (page 124)
Cajun Deep-Fried Turkey (page 138)
Bourbon Bombs (page 150)

ORANGE BOWL

Miami Dolphinfish Steaks (page 108) or Barbecued Chicken (page 94)
Black-Eyed Pea Salsa (page 40)
One-Two Punch (page 143)
Piña Colada Cake (page 54)

NASCAR

INDY 500 SPREAD
Beer-Butt Chicken (page 98)
Grilled Corn on the Cob (page 58)
Spinach Artichoke Bread Bowl (page 36)
Chocolate Whiskey Pudding (page 52)

NEXTEL (WINSTON) CUP BLOWOUT
Carolina Pulled Pork (page 77)
Grilled Corn on the Cob (page 58)
Creamy Slaw (page 41)
Barbecue Beans (page 116)
Champion Chip Cookies (page 160)

DAYTONA 500 FEAST
Buttermilk Fried Chicken (page 164)
Smoky Rubbed Ribs (page 72)
Black-Eyed Pea Salsa (page 40)
Creamy Slaw (page 41)
Chipotle Pecans (page 158)

SOURCES FOR

Tailgating
GEAR

All kinds of retailers—from sporting goods stores to hardware stores—
now fill entire sections with tailgating gear. It's easy to find grills and coolers designed just for tailgaters. Here's where to get the stuff that's harder
to come by—like wild game meats, your favorite microbrews, tents, RV
rentals, and DJ equipment. To buy or rent equipment you don't see here,
check your local yellow pages or the Internet.

GENERAL GEAR

AMERICAN TAILGATERS ASSOCIATION

The first national tailgating club offers a beverage tub, eight-piece BBQ toolkit in carrying case, knife set, clothing, and other gear.
www.atatailgate.com
210-326-0451

THE AMERICAN TAILGATER COMPANY

Company offers cool gear like grilling irons to brand meat with your favorite logo; a speed marinator; portable rest room; padded bench to place on your tailgate; and canopies. Also carries the "Ultimate Tailgating System," an all-in-one setup that includes a 50,000 BTU gas grill, a refrigerator/freezer, stainless-steel sink, outlets for three appliances, and optional beer taps and umbrella ($5,795 with beer taps).
www.americantailgater.com
888-844-4263

BAGGO.COM

If you get tired of tossing the pigskin, try throwing bean bags instead. Call the company to get a custom-made game with your team's or tailgating club's logo.
www.baggo.com
888-323-1813

E-Z UP DIRECT

The most popular portable shelter. Choose from 17 different E-Z Up tents in various shapes and sizes. For some extra scratch, go all out with custom colors and graphics to really show your tailgating spirit.
www.ezupdirect.com
800-SHADE-ME (800-742-3363)

TAILGATEHQ.COM

NFL and NCAA helmet grills, keg grills, Freedom grills as seen on the cover, Baggo games, team-branded tents, E-Z Up tents, and Fan Brands, a cool barbecue grilling iron that allows you to brand your steak, chicken, or pork with your favorite football team logo or NASCAR driver number.
www.tailgateHQ.com
813-493-9890

TAILGATEPARTYSHOP.COM

Site offers a wide variety of tailgating goodies, with many items emblazoned with team logos. Selections include mud flaps, hitch covers, folding chairs, and serving trays.
www.tailgatepartyshop.com
877-TAL-GATE

TAILGATINGSUPPLIES.COM

Company carries a wide variety of gear to meet your tailgating needs. Offerings include car-antenna pendants and vehicle flags; flagpoles; coolers; whimsical grills (shaped like kegs and footballs); and team-logo stools and chairs.
www.tailgatingsupplies.com
260-492-9062

TEXAN TAILGATERS

The Texas-size spread of offerings from this company includes grills, smokers, and turkey fryers; and tables, chairs, and other accessories.

For the serious tailgating chef, the company also offers deluxe cooking equipment including the Greatmate Grill, which attaches to a 2-inch receiver behind your vehicle and features 340 square inches of cooking surface, with optional generator, refrigerator, and television. Prices start at $2,595.

The company also offers competition-size pit barbecues mounted on trailers, suitable for cooking for large crowds. Call for pricing.
www.texantailgaters.com
866-254-1431

GRILLS, TOOLS, AND ACCESSORIES

AMERICA'S BEST BARBECUE

Offers grills, smokers, sauces and rubs, coolers, patio heaters, shelters, and more.
www.americasbestbbq.com
800-814-6815

BARBECUE! BIBLE STORE

The site run by barbecue guru and author Steven Raichlen offers books; wood chips; and grilling accessories such as a rib rack, grilling baskets, a chimney starter, and drip pans.
www.barbecuebible.com

THE BARBECUE STORE

Wide array of gas, charcoal, and portable grills, wood-burning pits, and electric smokers; barbecue accessories such as grill racks, roasters, baskets, seasoning injectors, thermometers, grill covers, wood planks, lump charcoal, food, and much more.
www.barbecue-store.com
888-789-0650

BARBECUEWOOD.COM

Washington-based company will ship out wood chips, chunks, and pellets in varieties ranging from apple to mesquite to white oak (and wood from Jack Daniel's aging barrels, too). Also offers lump charcoal, planks for cooking fish, and other accessories.
www.barbecuewood.com
509-961-3420

CHARCOAL GRILL DEPOT

Offers a huge number of wood and charcoal grills, as well as accessories and specialty wood chips and chunks.
www.charcoalgrilldepot.com
877-743-2269

A COOK'S WARES

A well-chosen catalog of general cookware and high-quality barbecue tools, including spatulas, forks, turner-tongs, basting brushes, thermometers, marinade injectors, and heatproof gloves.
www.cookswares.com
800-915-9788

FREEDOM GRILL GRILLING SYSTEMS

Offers the Freedom Grill 100 (as seen on the cover), a 30,000 BTU stainless-steel grill mounted on an arm that fastens to a 2-inch receiver hitch behind your vehicle. The grill stays behind your vehicle on the way to the game, then swings out for cooking and locks back in place while you're at the game. $799.
www.freedomgrill.com
866-96-GRILL

GASGRILLSUPERSTORE.COM

As its name implies, this company offers gas grills in all styles, shapes, sizes, and prices. Many accessories, too.
www.gasgrillsuperstore.com
877-743-2269

THE HUBERT COMPANY

For the dedicated tailgater, a purveyor of commercial food service and catering items that come in handy such as heatproof silicone gloves, insulated food transport bags, and chafing dishes. Keep in mind that if you don't want to buy this sort of pricey catering equipment, you can usually rent it from a restaurant supply store. Check the yellow pages for a restaurant supply store near you.
www.hubert.com
800-543-7374

THE TOOL WIZARD

All sorts of nifty grilling accessories and food-preparation tools, including chile-pepper grills, tenderizing gadgets, and cutlery sets.
www.bbq-tools.com
800-630-TOOL

SPECIALTY ITEMS

BLENDERBLASTER

Offers a super-manly gas-powered blender with joystick or motorcycle-style throttle and aluminum treadplate base. Available with 2-cycle or 4-cycle motor. $319 to $549.
www.blenderblaster.com
414-352-1988

TAILGATOR

Company carries a 24 $\times$ 36-inch wooden table that attaches to 2-inch receiver hitch behind your vehicle or stands on a pedestal-type leg. Features four cup holders in corners. Available with NCAA or racing logos. $184.95 to $249.95.
www.tailgator.net
888-341-2050

FOOD AND DRINK

BROKEN ARROW RANCH

Texas-based mail-order game supplier offering packages and individual products, with selections including antelope and venison fillets, loin, kebabs, stew chunks, sausage, and ground meat.
www.brokenarrowranch.com
800-962-4263

CHOCOLATE SOURCE

A wide variety of good-quality chocolate chips, bars, and blocks.
www.chocolatesource.com
800-214-4926

GAME SALES INTERNATIONAL

Colorado food supplier offers gourmet ravioli filled with buffalo, pheasant, boar, and other meats; New Zealand lamb; wild boar; pheasant; and wild mushrooms.
www.gamesalesintl.com
800-729-2090

MO HOTTA MO BETTA

Offers a huge array of hot sauces, barbecue sauces, spices, and snacks.
www.mohotta.com
800-462-3220

PENZEYS SPICES

Massive array of good-quality and hard-to-find spices and seasoning blends.
www.penzeys.com
800-741-7787

SEATTLE'S FINEST EXOTIC MEATS

Wide array of meats include alligator tail steak, semi-boneless snapping turtle meat, llama patties, kangaroo sausage, and whole rattlesnake. Company also offers exotic poultry and seafood, and sauces.
www.exoticmeats.com
800-680-4375

WORLD BEER DIRECT

Introduce your closest friends to a new beer each month. Choose from five beer-of-the-month clubs, which will send different assortments of imports and/or micro-brews to your door. Also offers cigar- and wine-of-the-month clubs.
www.worldbeerdirect.com
800-609-ALES

TAILGATING TRAILERS

ALL AMERICAN TAILGATER

Specializing in customized, fully enclosed tow-behind tailgating trailers. All trailers feature keg refrigerator, food refrigerator and freezer, microwave, sink, storage space, 5-disc DVD/CD player, surround-sound stereo, outside speakers, side awning, at least two TVs, satellite dish and receiver, toilet, and more. More equipped trailers come with more floor space, full bathroom, fold-down beds, and other options. Base prices range from $34,900 to $48,390.
www.allamericantailgater.com
866-423-9251

TAILGATER PARTY TRAILERS

Open-air, tow-behind trailer includes grill, tap for beer or other drinks, stainless-steel sink, radio/CD/stereo with speakers, storage area, and seating area for eight covered by retractable canopy. Trailers are available for rental from dealers around the country.
www.tailgaterpartytrailers.com
866-238-9681

VEHICLE RENTALS

CRUISE AMERICA RV RENTAL AND SALES

Rent a mobile home to tailgate in true comfort. Company rents from locations throughout America, including Alaska, and from a few locations in Canada.
www.cruiseamerica.com
800-671-8042

RECREATION VEHICLE RENTAL ASSOCIATION

Offers a directory of RV rental outlets across America.
www.rvra.org
703-591-7130

FAN GEAR

BEST SPORTS APPAREL

Pick up a jersey, shirt, sweatshirt, jacket, or other clothing item to support your favorite NFL team. Site also offers links to stuff for fans of baseball, hockey, basketball, and NASCAR.

www.nflstore.net

800-694-0060

FANSEDGE

Find apparel, tailgating gear, and other merchandise bearing the logo and colors of your favorite NFL, NBA, Major League Baseball, NHL, and NCAA team, or favorite NASCAR driver.

www.fansedge.com

877-965-3955

NASCAR.COM SUPERSTORE

If you need an upholstered NASCAR-themed sofa, chair, or ottoman to bring out on race day, you can find more than a dozen here. Also shop for apparel, collectibles, and miniatures.

www.nascar.com

866-290-4569

Acknowledgments

I HAD ONE OVERRIDING RULE FOR THE FOOD IN THIS BOOK: every recipe must contain either alcohol or chile peppers—or both. For months, as I fine-tuned the recipes, I religiously followed this commandment (especially the alcohol part). Then, one day, this rule was finally broken, as all rules eventually are. Nonetheless, I would like to thank my liver for its strength and endurance throughout recipe development, particularly during the marathon re-testing of Long Island Iced Teas.

Many other sacrifices were made as I wrote the book, quite a few of them by my wife, Christine, who picked up the slack of my household duties. Christine, you are a saint for putting up with the crazy hours of a writer, the endless dirty dishes of a recipe developer, and the messy paper stacks of a fanatical researcher. Thank you for living through this book with grace. And for your razor-sharp taste buds! Big bear hugs also to my kids, August and Maddox, for taking "No Thank You" bites, making me laugh, and keeping me going. Go Steelers! What a fútbol?

A huge thank-you to all the tailgaters who shared their recipes, team spirit, and parking lot wisdom, especially Joe Cahn, Mike Hammett, Becky Barker, Big John and Linda Gavin, Russ Stevenson, Sean Deegan, Ken Johnson, Roy Taylor, Mike Mason, Keith and Elizabeth Moodie, Jack McDavid, the Baltimore Ravens' SWAT Team, Matt Andrews, Randy Pierce, Craig and Karen Cordell, Marc Menkin, and Jo Anne and Jimmy Hlavac.

For great barbecuing and grilling advice, a tip of the tongs to Steven Raichlen, Cheryl Alters Jamison, and Bill Jamison. I've learned a great deal from each of you.

My foodie friends Sharon Sanders, Raghavan Iyer, and Normand LeClair have been there with steady support throughout this project. I am grateful for your friendship, wisdom, and advice over the years.

A round of thank-yous to all the other recipe testers and tasters, including Selene Yeager, Chris and Lisa Neyen, Tom Aczel, Michele Raes, Kim and Andrew Brubaker, Bridget Doherty, Cindy Mack, Jack Croft, and Dan and Stephanie Albanese. The boys at South Mountain Cycles bike and coffee shop, Taylor and Bowman (and Röbi), deserve a special nod. You guys gave up your taste buds and your counter space for months of recipe tastings. I owe you big time for that. Put it on my tab. While you're at it, I'll take a Dirty McGurty to go!

Thanks to George Devault of Pheasant Hill Farm, Rod Wieder of Backyard Bison, and all the other local food producers at the Emmaus Farmers Market. I am deeply grateful for your commitment to responsible farming and good-quality food. I'm lucky to be able to work with such great raw materials.

To Kevin and Susan Ireland, thank you for your hospitality, taste-testing, and friendship during my Florida research trip. And to my faithful research cohorts Dave Pryor, Bill Doherty, and Dale Mack: you guys rock! Who else would travel with a crazy food writer carrying a beach cooler full of marinating meat on a plane? Thanks for being great recipe tasters and supreme sports fans. A special shout out to Dave for helping with the menus section. And, yo, Wiley and Doris Horton, when's our next Gators tailgate? I gotta check out your new RV!

To the always cheerful John Largent at the American Tailgaters Association, God bless you for supporting all things tailgating. I also appreciate the research help of Leslie Wheeler at the Hearth, Patio, and Barbecue Association, Carrie Lucas at Weber-Stephen Products, and the folks at the Iowa Beef Industry Council, the National Chicken Council, and the American Institute for Cancer Research.

Mark Bernstein, Chris Warner, and Charlie Maher enriched this book with their historical and psychological perspectives on American football. To all three of you, thank you for keeping a scholarly eye on the evolving tradition of tailgating in America.

I owe a supersize debt of gratitude to Eric Metcalf for his invaluable help with interviews and research. Thanks, Eric, for making me laugh out loud during the dog days of writing.

This book would have never come to pass if not for my agent, Lisa Ekus. You are such a joy to work with. Thank you for sharing your generous spirit, infectious smile, and infinite Rolodex.

A special thank-you to editor extraordinaire Jennifer Josephy, who let me run with her ideas for this book. Jennifer, your gentle patience is matched only by your sharp and discerning mind. A nod of gratitude to art director Umi Kenyon for going the extra mile to get a great cover photo. And thanks to the rest of the staff at Broadway who turned the manuscript into a real, live, hold-in-your-hands book.

A quick bow of gratitude to Shangy's, the impeccably stocked and cheerfully run beer store located three miles from my house. This place should be called Shangri-La. I'm in beer heaven every time I step in!

Finally, to Ronald Joachim, who passed from this world before he could taste my Chipotle-Bourbon Ribs: thanks for teaching me how to tend a fire, Dad. You would have loved those ribs.

Index

mango-orange salsa
>Miami dolphinfish steaks with, 108-9

maple-rosemary planked salmon, 104-5

marinades, 18-20

meat
>brining, 20, 22
>
>marinades, 18-20
>
>spice rubs, 22
>
>*See also* beef; buffalo; pork; sausage(s); venison stew

meatball hero, 118-19

menu planning, 9, 173-78

Miami Dolphins, 56, 103

mimosas, 143

Minnesota Vikings, 121

mocha madness, 150-51

Moodie, Keith and Elizabeth, 127

Moss, Randy, 121

N

NASCAR tailgating, 8, 81

New England Patriots, 107

New York Giants, 56, 127

New York Jets, 56, 65

noodle salad, Chinese, 46-47

nuts
>chipotle pecans, 158

O

Oakland Raiders, 65, 86, 103

Ohio State University, 7, 50

olives
>tapenade, 34
>
>tomato-olive goat cheese tart, 162-63

one-two punch, 143

onions
>grilled, fajitas with, 83
>
>Philly cheesesteak with, 122-23
>
>orange-mango salsa, Miami dolphinfish steaks
>>with, 108-9
>
>Orme, Len, 3

P

panini, chicken pesto, 64-65

Parisi, Mike, 2

pasta salads
>Chinese noodle salad, 46-47
>
>pesto tortellini salad, 48

peanut butter
>buckeye candy, 50
>
>Chinese noodle salad, 46-47

pecans
>bourbon bombs, 159
>
>champion chip cookies, 160-61
>
>chipotle pecans, 158

peppers, hot. *See* chiles, chile powder; chili; chipotle
>chiles; salsa; spice rubs

peppers, sweet
>grilled, fajitas with, 83
>
>Philly cheesesteak with, 122-23
>
>*See also* chiles, chile powder; chipotle chiles

pesto, basil, 35
>chicken pesto panini, 64-65
>
>pesto Gorgonzola grilled pizza, 62-63
>
>pesto tortellini salad, 48

Philadelphia Eagles, 2-3, 3-4, 56, 127

Phillips, Stephanie, 2-3

Philly cheesesteak, 122-23

Pierce, Randy, 107

pineapple
>piña colada cake, 54-55
>
>relish, swordfish steaks with, 106-7

pine nuts
>basil pesto, 35
>
>tapenade with, 34

pizza
>grilled calzones, 66-67
>
>pesto Gorgonzola grilled pizza, 62-63

planked salmon, maple-rosemary, 104-5

pork
>Carolina pulled pork, 77-79
>
>chipotle-bourbon ribs, 74-76
>
>meatball hero, 118-19